THE
CRIMINAL
RECORDS
BOOK

WARREN SIEGEL

legal editor
STEPHEN ELIAS

please read this

We have done our best to give you useful and accurate information concerning criminal records. But please be aware that laws and procedures are constantly changing and are subject to differing interpretations. You have the responsibility to check all material you read here before relying on it. If your lawyer gives you different advice than you read here, please check it out carefully. Of necessity, neither Nolo Press nor the author makes any guarantees concerning the information in this publication or the use to which it is put.

nolo press   **950 parker street**   **berkeley ca 94710**

important

Nolo Press is committed to keeping its books up-to-date. Each new printing, whether or not it is called a new edition, has been revised to reflect the latest law changes. This book was printed and updated on the last date indicated below. Before you rely on information in it, you might wish to call Nolo Press (415) 549-1976 to check whether a later printing or edition has been issued.

printing history

New "**Printing**" means there have been some minor changes, but usually not enough so that people will need to trade in or discard an earlier printing of the same edition. Obviously, this is a judgment call and any change, no matter how minor, might affect you.

New "**Edition**" means one or more major, or a number of minor, law changes since the previous edition.

First Edition	June 1983
Second Edition	September 1986
Third Edition	October 1989
Second Printing	April 1990

Legal Research	Stephen Elias
Illustrations	Linda Allison
Production	Stephanie Harolde
Book Design	Jackie Clark
Cover Design	Amy Ihara
Printing	Delta Lithograph

ISBN 0-87337-116-X
Library of Congress Catalog Card No.: 83-61729

acknowledgements

My thanks and gratitude go out to all of those individuals who shared information with me, reviewed the manuscript and who worked on the book.

I would like to gratefully acknowledge the major contribution of Stéphen Elias, whose thorough editing added considerable focus and clarity to this book. If you find this book easy and enjoyable to read, Steve desires much of the credit.

Many thanks to Santa Clara County Superior Court Judge Leonard P. Edwards, Peter E. Sheehan, attorney with the Legal Aid Society of Alameda County, San Mateo County probation officers David Anderson and Vern Phillips, and Contra Costa County probation officer Richard Calicura, who took the time to review the manuscript and offer helpful suggestions and comments.

Thanks, too, to the following individuals, organizations and agencies who responded to my initial request for information and advice and provided me with forms and local procedures: probation departments of Alameda, Fresno, Sacramento and San Mateo counties and the Federal probation department for Northern and Central Districts of California; public defenders offices of Los Angeles and San Francisco counties; California Department of Justice Record Review Unit; National Organization for the Reform of Marijuana Laws; Assemblymember Thomas Hannigan; former Assemblymember Walter Karabian; and Bryant Byrnes, attorney.

Finally I want to thank all the people at Nolo Press who offered their support for his book and to those who worked on the production, including Keija Kimura, Stephanie Harolde, and Linda Allison.

I also want to thank Barbara Oaks, who had the thankless task of listening to my dictation and typing the first draft of this book.

about the author

Warren Siegel is staff attorney for Jacoby and Meyers in Pleasant Hills. Since graduating from Golden Gate University Law School in San Francisco in 1974, he has also worked for Marin County's Criminal Justice Planning Department and as a Deputy Public Defender in San Francisco. In addition to writing this book, he is the co-author of the Nolo Press publication *How To Modify and Collect Child Support in California,* which was first published in 1987.

RECYCLE YOUR OUT-OF-DATE BOOKS & GET 25% OFF YOUR NEXT PURCHASE!

Using an old edition can be dangerous if information in it is wrong. Unfortunately, laws and legal procedures change often. To help you keep up to date we extend this offer. If you cut out and deliver to us the title portion of the cover of any old Nolo book we'll give you a 25% discount off the retail price of any new Nolo book. For example, if you have a copy of TENANT'S RIGHTS, 4th edition and want to trade it for the latest CALIFORNIA MARRIAGE AND DIVORCE LAW, send us the TENANT'S RIGHTS cover and a check for the current price of MARRIAGE & DIVORCE, less a 25% discount. Information on current prices and editions is listed in the NOLO NEWS. Generally speaking, any book more than two years old is of questionable value. Books more than four or five years old are a menace. This offer is to individuals only.

OUT OF DATE = DANGEROUS

CRIM 4/90

table of contents

introduction

chapter 1

criminal records: what do they mean?

chapter 2

background about criminal records

chapter 3

how to find your record cleaning remedy

chapter 4

juvenile delinquency and status offense records

appendix

introduction

Have you ever:

- Been arrested?
- Been convicted of a crime?
- Been found delinquent in juvenile court?

If you answered "yes" to any of these questions, you have a criminal record. If your criminal record took place in California, this book will help you. If it occurred in another state, you will need to locate information specific to your state.

Having a record can be a drag. It's a little like getting tar on your feet—the main stuff can be washed off but the stain seems to last much longer. In an old American classic, a woman was branded with a scarlet "A" to remind the townsfolk of her sin. These days, modern communications and computers do the branding for us. If you have ever been arrested, convicted, or put through the juvenile court process, your "scarlet letter" will be found somewhere inside a filing cabinet or in the electronic patterns of a computer, just waiting to bear witness to your past indiscretions.

Criminal records can prevent you from getting jobs, going in the military, running for public office, obtaining professional or commercial licenses, and securing credit. If you're ever in court again, your criminal record may lead to harsher punishment if you're convicted. In short, having a criminal record can really hang you up.

Although you may have been represented by a lawyer and helped by a probation officer as part of your initial contact(s) with the criminal justice system, they have probably moved on to other cases. This means, if you want to do something about improving your record and restoring your good name, you need to take the initiative.

Minimizing the effects of your criminal record will leave you a lot better off than you are at present. In many cases, pursuing your record cleaning remedy will allow you to answer "no" to questions about past arrests and convictions. In others, you'll be able to compete for jobs without your "criminal" background being raised. In just about every case, you'll be better off if you ever land in court again.

It's easier to get rid of some kinds of records than others. Juvenile records and records of marijuana possession offenses can be totally destroyed, for example, whereas felony conviction records can only be changed for certain limited purposes. In all, the law provides a number of different remedies for different types of records and these remedies vary in their effectiveness.

Regardless of what kind of record you have, however, we strongly believe you should clean it up as much as possible. You have nothing to lose and everything to gain.

If you're interested in trying to do something about your California record, here is what this book provides.

In Chapter 1, we'll give you a little information about how your record can adversely affect you. Unfortunately, you probably already know much of this.

In Chapter 2 we tell you what your "record" consists of, how to get a copy of it, and how to correct any inaccuracies you happen to discover.

In Chapter 3 we will be asking you some questions about your contact with the criminal justice system. Depending on your answers, we will tell you to keep reading or directly refer you to another chapter. Each of the chapters after Chapter 3 covers a specific record improving remedy. Some will apply to your situation, many won't. Chapter 3, therefore, is like a map or directory, designed to get you to the chapter which will best meet your needs.

In each chapter covering a specific remedy, we'll be asking you some more questions, just to make sure you've come to the right place. If you have, we'll then guide you step-by-step through the process necessary to seal, expunge or destroy your record (depending on what type it is). If it turns out that the particular remedy doesn't fit your situation, we'll refer you to the right one.

So long as you take it one step at a time, it isn't difficult. Even devout followers of Murphy's Law, which provides that everything that can go wrong will go wrong, should be pleasantly surprised. In each of our "how to do it" chapters, we explain in more detail the benefits of the remedy being covered and how you can respond to questions about your record, but we want to reassure you here that we believe the benefits to definitely be worth the small hassle involved.

chapter 1 ─────────────

criminal records:
what do they mean?

A. How Can Your Criminal Record Hurt You?

IF NOBODY EVER ASKED questions about your past, then this book wouldn't be necessary. If, however, you've filled out an application for a job or occupational license, you know there are almost always questions about your possible criminal background. A "yes" answer to any of these questions often has extremely negative results.

The following several paragraphs will help you understand which questions can legally be asked. More important, it will tell you how to respond.

1. Is it legal to be asked if you've ever been arrested?

If you were arrested and charged with a crime and then your case was dismissed or you won at trial, we have good news for you. Since you're presumed innocent until proven guilty (by being convicted), California law limits the situations when you can even be asked about arrests. For example, most prospective employers cannot ask about your arrest record. The only ones who can are law enforcement agencies, public education

institutions, and certain health facilities. If any other employment application asks about arrests, the chances are good that the law is being violated and you don't have to answer. In fact, you may even be entitled to sue for damages (Labor Code §432.7b).

Caution: If you find a question about "arrests" on an employment application, you need to decide whether to answer the question truthfully, possibly lose the job and then sue for damages, or lie, get the job, and hope the employer will never find out, or will keep you on after you point out what the law provides. Hopefully, most employers comply with the law and you won't be faced with this choice.

2. How should you answer questions about arrests if your case was diverted?

If your case was "diverted" out of the criminal justice system and you successfully completed the diversion "program," your record won't reflect an arrest but only a "detention." Thus, if asked about prior arrests you can answer "no."[1] However, you

---

[1] Penal Code §§1000.5, 1000.10, 1001.33, 1001.55, 1001.75.

should be aware that detentions associated with diverted cases are listed differently on your rap sheet than detentions where charges were never filed, and some probation officers, judges, and prosecuting attorneys are more suspicious of you if you later get into trouble again.

3. How should you answer questions about cases related to marijuana possession and use?

If you were arrested or convicted of certain marijuana related crimes, and two years have passed since the case ended, your conviction (or arrest) is no longer considered to be "accurate, relevant, timely or complete for any purpose by any agency or person" (Health & Safety Code §11361.7a) and your arrest or conviction for these marijuana-related offenses needn't be disclosed when any question is asked about your prior criminal record (Health & Safety Code §11361.7c). Most employers shouldn't ask about these types of cases on employment applications (Labor Code §432.8). Offenses involving sale, cultivation, or possession for sale aren't covered by this remedy. We discuss the remedy for getting marijuana convictions off your record in detail in Chapter 6.

4. How should you answer questions about arrests if your case involved public drunkenness?

If you were arrested for being intoxicated in public, and no criminal charges were filed in court, or if you were arrested for being under the influence of narcotics, drugs, or restricted dangerous drugs, and you were taken to a hospital for treatment instead of being charged with a crime, your arrest is considered a "detention" (Penal Code §849c) and you can answer "no" to questions about prior arrests. The California Department of Justice (the main record keeping agency in California) doesn't keep records for these kinds of cases (Penal Code §13153).

5. How should you answer questions about federal drug possession cases?

If you were arrested and charged with possession of "controlled substances" (certain drugs) and your case was dismissed in Federal Court under procedures described in Chapter 11, you can answer "no" to any questions about your criminal convictions (21 United States Code §844). This law was repealed, effective November 1, 1986.

6. How should you answer questions about juvenile cases?

If you "sowed some wild oats" as a kid and have a juvenile court record, you haven't been convicted of a crime or arrested for a crime (Welfare & Institutions Code §203). Why? Because, juvenile courts aren't part of the criminal justice system and terms like arrest and conviction simply aren't used (unless your case was transferred from juvenile court to adult court after a "fitness" hearing).

Of course, when the police officer grabbed you and took you to the police station you may have felt like you were being arrested, but fortunately, for purposes of answering questions about arrests, you can answer "no." Similarly, even if the court decided that you were guilty of what you were charged with, you weren't convicted and can therefore answer "no" to questions about convictions.

Some federal government agencies, employers or armed services don't recognize state law on juvenile record sealing. If you're applying for employment with any of these agencies, you may need to disclose your juvenile court matter. The same caution should apply if you apply for employment with the government in a state other than California or private employers who require federal government security clearance as a condition of employment.

B. How Can a Criminal Convictions Record Harm You?

1. The Condition of Being an "Ex-Felon"

First, if you were convicted of a crime, it will make a lot of difference whether the crime was a misdemeanor or a felony. We discuss in Chapter 3 how to tell the difference. Unfortunately, if it was a felony, things will be more difficult for you. Many bad effects result from being an "ex-felon." For example, if you've been convicted of a felony you cannot:

a) Become a law enforcement officer with any law enforcement agency in California (Government Code §1029a);

b) Enlist in any branch of the U.S. Armed Services, unless your case fits into a "meritorious exception" (10 U.S.C. 504);

c) Serve on a jury (Cal. Constitution VII, §8; C.C.P. 199; Penal Code §893b3; 28 U.S.C. 1865);

d) Vote when you're on parole (Cal. Constitution II, §4);

e) Possess concealable firearms (Penal Code §§12021a, 12560; 18 U.S.C. §§922h and 1202a);

f) Hold certain categories of federal jobs if your felony conviction was for civil disorder or rioting crimes (5 U.S.C. §7313);

g) Hold certain California public offices (Cal. Constitution VII §8b; Government Code §§1021, 1097); and

h) Get your juvenile records sealed, as described in Chapters 4 and 5.

If your felony conviction is for a crime where the facts prove your unfitness to have future custody and control of a child, it can be the basis for terminating your parental rights (Civil Code §232a4).

If you're going to testify in a court case, your felony conviction may often be introduced to attack your honesty as a witness. This is more likely to occur if you testify in a criminal case (Cal. Constitution I, §28f).

In criminal cases, felony convictions for crimes of "moral turpitude" may, subject to the trial court's discretion, be used against you, even if the immoral trait is other than dishonesty. "Moral turpitude" crimes have been defined by the California Supreme Court in *People v. Castro* (1985) 38 Cal. [3d] 301 as those which show a general readiness to do evil or which evinces any character trait that can reasonably be characterized as immoral.

2. Licensing and Employment Problems

There are many occupations that require a license before you can lift a finger. Certain types of convictions may hinder you in obtaining the license. Further, if you're already licensed, a subsequent conviction for certain crimes can get your license yanked.

The people who issue licenses and regulate your career have been given the power to inquire into the circumstances surrounding any crime you were convicted of. If they decide that the crime was "substantially related" to the requirements of the particular career involved (i.e., if the crime involved theft and the career involves private investigator work), they have the power to deny you the license or impose discipline on you if you're already licensed. Unfortunately, it isn't always easy to predict whether a particular licensing agency will find a crime "substantially related" to the requirements of the work in question.

Here are some examples of cases where the court concluded there is a substantial relationship between the criminal conviction and the qualifications, functions and duties of the profession:

- A conviction for marijuana possession may lead to the loss of a real estate license [*Golde v. Fox* (1979) 98 Cal. App. [3d] 167];
- A federal conspiracy conviction may lead to the loss of a real estate license [*Arneson v. Fox* (1980) 28 Cal. [3d] 440];
- Income tax evasion conviction may lead to the loss of a physician's license [*Windham v. Board of Medical Quality Assurance* (1980) 104 Cal. App. [3d] 461].

Here, on the other hand, are examples where the court concluded that no "substantial relationship" existed:

- Child molesting conviction may not lead to the loss of a license to sell cars [*Brewer v. DMV* (1979) 93 Cal. App. [3d] 358];
- Cocaine distribution conviction may not lead to the loss of a real estate license [*Brandt v. Fox* (1979) 90 Cal. App. [3d] 737].

Note: As you can see from these examples, one court may decide that a cocaine distributor is entitled to a real estate license where another court will deny a license to a marijuana possessor. There's just no sure way to predict the outcome of any particular case. That's why it's a good idea to eliminate your record as much as the law will allow.

In addition to licensing problems, your conviction may harm you when you look for a job. Once a potential employer learns of your criminal record, it may be all over. And even if it doesn't make a difference with many employers, you may lose out because you can't get a bond and the job you're applying for requires one (as in the case of cashiers, insurance salesmen, and bank tellers). This is especially true if your offense was honesty-related. Some convicted felons may qualify to get a bond from the California Employment Development Department.

3. Increasing Punishment in Future Criminal Cases

Convictions can be used to impose harsher sentences for future crimes and in some cases mandate jail time upon a second offense. Cleaning up your record will often prevent this kind of double punishment.

4. Registration With Police Department

If you were convicted of certain criminal offenses relating to lewd conduct or other sex related crimes, you'll be required to register with the police department in the city where you live and with the California Department of Justice.[2] If you move, you must notify the police within 10 days (Penal Code §290). Registration consists of a written statement, fingerprints, and a photo. Only regularly employed peace officers and law enforcement officers have access to this information. The duty to register as a sex offender is a lifelong responsibility unless you use the remedies described in this book. Using the juvenile record sealing procedure described in Chapter 4 may lead to a more rapid destruction of these records by the Department of Justice and other agencies that have records relating to the registration requirement (Penal Code §290d4).

Persons convicted of certain narcotics offenses must also register with the local law enforcement agency within 30 days after moving to any city or county (Health & Safety Code §§11590a, 11594). This duty to register ends five years after discharge from prison, release from jail, or termination of probation or parole, unless you can get your conviction dismissed using the procedure described in Chapter 7 before the five-year period ends.

---

[2]This registration requirement was held to be unconstitutional as it applied to misdemeanor convictions for Penal Code §647(a). *In Re Reed* (1983) 33 Cal. [3d] 914.

5. Traffic Cases

If any subject deserves the attention of this book, it would seem to be traffic cases. Between the point system (where you lose your license after accumulating a certain amount of points caused by tickets) and mandatory jail time and license suspension or restriction for second offense drunk driving, the motor vehicle laws are heavily dependent on records. Unfortunately, none of the remedies available at the present can be used to clean up your motor vehicle record (when it comes to traffic offenses). For more information on these topics, see Chapters 15 and 8 of *Fight Your Ticket,* a Nolo Press book by Dave Brown.

6. Immigration Consequences

If you're not a U.S. citizen, a criminal conviction on your record may lead to a number of unpleasant consequences. You could be deported from the country, excluded if you try to re-enter, or be disqualified from becoming a citizen.

The type of crimes that lead to the most problems are moral turpitude crimes, drug- or sex-related offenses, weapons possession, prostitution, and certain other crimes.

For moral turpitude crimes, using the remedies discussed in this book will prevent the convictions from being used to deport you.

If you're convicted of a moral turpitude crime, you can also be protected from deportation if the sentencing judge agrees to sign an order called a "Judicial Recommendation Against Deportation" within 30 days of the time of sentencing.

None of these protections apply to narcotics or any other convictions not involving moral turpitude.

Due to these serious consequences, California law (Penal Code §1016.5) requires the court to give all non-citizens special warnings before a guilty plea to any crime is accepted.

C. Conclusion

WE'VE GIVEN YOU THIS short catalogue of the effects of a criminal record not to depress you, but only to remind you of something you surely already know: having a criminal record can seriously interfere with your life. If you agree, and want to do something about your record, the following chapters will help you find the right remedy for your case and will provide you detailed guidance every step of the way.

However, keep one thought in mind. Some of the remedies discussed here are more effective than others. Very few promise complete relief. Nevertheless, some relief in this area is far better than none.

chapter 2 ————————————

background about criminal records

YOU PROBABLY HAVE NO IDEA what your criminal record looks like, where it's kept, or who can look at it. If you wanted a copy, you most likely haven't a clue as to how you would get one. In this chapter, we'll give you some background on these topics so you'll have a better idea of what having a criminal record actually means. Also, we'll tell you how to get copies of yours.

Note: If you're not particularly interested in this information and want to restore your good name by the straightest route possible, then skip this chapter and go directly to Chapter 3. That chapter will steer you to the right part of the book for sealing or expunging your criminal record.

A. What Is a Criminal Record?

AS SOON AS YOU'RE TAKEN into custody by the police, you not only lose your freedom, but obtain a criminal record as well. You surely remember having your "mug shots" and fingerprints taken by the police. In addition, your record will contain other information about you as a person and a summary of how your encounter with the authorities ended (Penal Code §§13102, 13125). This includes a summary of arrests, including the charges and sentence, fingerprint identification number, Criminal Identification Information (CII)

number, F.B.I. number, social security number, and California driver's license number. This information is frequently called a "rap sheet."

Once a record is started by the police department, the information is also sent to state and federal agencies that keep criminal records. All California criminal records are kept by the State Department of Justice, while national criminal records are kept by the F.B.I. You're entitled to have the record contain accurate information. Once your case ends, whether by conviction or dismissal, the court must inform the Department of Justice within 30 days, and if your case is dismissed by the court, the reasons must be stated (Penal Code §13151.1).

Of course, even though you're entitled to accurate records, this doesn't mean that they are maintained accurately. There are numerous stories about the failure of the Department of Justice to update criminal records to show dismissals, etc., and the F.B.I. is apparently even worse in this area. The increasing reliance on computers means that records can be updated more quickly and accurately on the one hand, but that lots of errors can be made more quickly on the other. A little later in this chapter we tell you how to check your criminal record for accuracy, both before undertaking the remedies outlined in this book and after.

B. Who Can Look at Your Criminal Record?

YOUR CRIMINAL RECORD may only be released to a restricted group of individuals or agencies. However, as you might expect, most agencies tied into the criminal justice system (police, courts, prosecutors, probation and parole departments, and even public defenders) and public agencies or officials who issue professional or occupational licenses or check employment applications do have access to your criminal record. In addition, if you're applying for a job as a police officer, or to work in a jail, certain health facilities, or in certain public utility facilities, your record may be checked by your potential employer (Penal Code §§11105, 13300).

If the wrong people are given access to your records, there are criminal penalties and you may have a civil action for damages as well (Penal Code §§11141-3, 13302-4).

When you apply for a job, your potential employer cannot require you to get a copy of your criminal record as a condition of employment (Penal Code §§11125, 13326).

Juvenile court records also may be released to a restricted group of individuals or agencies including the minor and his or her parents or guardian. And if the minor committed certain violent crimes or narcotics offenses, school officials will be notified (Welfare & Institutions Code §827).

C. How to Get a Copy of Your Criminal Record

YOU CAN GET A COPY of your criminal record so you can see what's on it and check to make sure it's accurate. Here are the procedures for obtaining each type of record.

1. F.B.I. Records

You can request your record from the F.B.I. by sending them a note asking for it, along with the following biographical information: 1) your name; 2) date and place of birth; 3) a set of fingerprints; and 4) a $14 fee (certified check or money order payable to the Treasury of the United States). You should send this information directly to the F.B.I., Identification Division, Washington D.C. 20537. Any request for waiver of the fee shall include a claim and proof of indigence. Contact the F.B.I. for how to do this.

2. California Records

You can get a copy of your state criminal record from the California Department of Justice by filling out the form entitled "Application to Obtain Copy of State Summary Criminal History Record." A copy of this form appears on the next page. In the Appendix we provide a blank form for you to fill in and use. If you need extra copies of this form, they should be available at your local police or sheriffs' departments, or you can write to the California Department of Justice and request additional forms.

State of California
DEPARTMENT OF JUSTICE

APPLICATION TO OBTAIN COPY OF STATE SUMMARY CRIMINAL HISTORY RECORD

California Penal Code Sections 11120 through 11127 (see reverse side) afford persons concerning whom a State Summary Criminal History Record is maintained in the files of the California Bureau of Criminal Identification the opportunity to obtain a copy of the record compiled from such files and refute any erroneous or inaccurate information contained therein.

Submission of the requested information is necessary as it will be used to determine if a record exists. Failure to supply this information may prevent this agency from providing you with a copy of your record. This application will be retained in your record folder if one exists. The Chief of the Bureau of Criminal Identification, California Department of Justice, is responsible for the maintenance of the information. The mailing address is P.O. Box 903417, Sacramento, California, 94203-4170, telephone number (916) 739-5140.

Any criminal record existing concerning you will be forwarded via mail or other appropriate means agreed to by you and the Department.

The undersigned hereby applies to obtain a copy of his/her State Criminal History Record:

(TYPE OR PRINT)

Applicant's Name _____
                  LAST NAME   FIRST NAME   MIDDLE NAME

Also known as
(or maiden name) _____
                  LAST NAME   FIRST NAME   MIDDLE NAME

Mailing Address _____
                  NUMBER   STREET

                  _____
                  CITY   STATE   ZIP CODE

Date of Birth ____/____/____   Telephone Number _____
               MONTH DAY YEAR   (Area Code) (8 a.m. - 5 p.m.)

If you wish this record forwarded to someone other than yourself, or if you wish this record mailed to an address different than the one listed above, complete the following:

Name _____   Title _____

Mailing Address _____
                  NUMBER   STREET

                  _____
                  CITY   STATE   ZIP CODE

X _____   _____
SIGNATURE OF APPLICANT   DATE

A standard fingerprint form or fingerprint form BID-7 with the applicant's fingerprints imprinted theron, containing all requested information, must accompany this application.

A fee of twenty dollars ($20.00) in the form of a U.S. Money Order, Certified Check, or Cashier's Check made payable to the California Department of Justice must accompany this application when forwarded to the Department of Justice. If you are indigent, a declaration of inability to pay the required fee will be forwarded for your signature upon request.

BCID 8705 (Rev. 1/86)

This completed application, a set of finger-prints, and a $20 fee should be sent to the California Department of Justice at the address listed at the top of the form. If you're unable to pay this fee without "impairing your obligation" to pay for the "common necessities of life," sign the "Application for Waiver of Fee." A blank form is provided in the Appendix.

APPLICATION AND DECLARATION FOR WAIVER OF
FEE FOR OBTAINING HISTORY RECORD

I, the undersigned, declare that I'm unable to pay the fee to obtain a copy of my criminal history record without impairing my obligation to meet the common necessities of life.

I declare under penalty of perjury that the foregoing is true and correct and was signed at _____,
California, on _____, 19__.

_____
Declarant

BCID 8690

As soon as the Department receives all of this information, they'll check their records to see if there's a criminal record for the person who's requesting it. If such a record does exist, it will be sent to either the applicant or the person designated by the applicant at the bottom of the application as the person to whom the record should be sent.

Important Note: The California Department of Justice has an ongoing program of destroying records after a given length of time. Records for certain marijuana offenses, for example, are destroyed after two years, and records of misdemeanor arrests without convictions are discarded after five. Misdemeanor convictions, felony arrests and most juvenile delinquency cases are gone after seven years. Therefore, it might happen that when you request your record, you may receive a response that it doesn't exist. That's fine as far as the Criminal Justice Department goes, but you still "have a record" for other purposes and should undertake the appropriate remedy to get it sealed, expunged, or destroyed, depending on the type of record.

3. Local Criminal Records

You can either obtain or look at a copy of your local criminal record at the police department responsible for your arrest or the county or city agency that keeps criminal records. Procedures used by the various law enforcement agencies vary throughout the state. Some are very efficient at finding and weeding out old records, while others aren't.

Each one of these local agencies has its own application form. They may require a set of fingerprints and a fee of up to $25. If you're unable to pay this fee without "impairing your obligation" to pay for the "common necessities of life," sign the Application for Waiver of Fee that appears in the following pages. A blank form is provided in the Appendix for your use.

Once the local agency receives your completed application, they'll check their records to

see if there's a local criminal record for the person requesting it. If so, you'll either be sent a copy or notified to come look at it.

4. Juvenile Court Records

If your case started and ended in a juvenile court, you can obtain all the court records associated with it. However, you must wait until five years have passed since the court was finished with you (sometimes referred to as "jurisdiction ending"). We suggest you check with your lawyer or probation officer to determine when to start counting this five year period.

Once it has passed, you simply give the court your name, date of birth, and your case number. Any court exhibits that are part of your file will be destroyed and your record handed to you. Once you have the record, your case is "deemed never to have occurred" and you can deny ever being involved with it if later asked (Welfare & Institutions Code §826a).

Note: We suggest you read Chapter 4 for more information on how to get your juvenile records sealed. If your records are ordered sealed by the court, all agencies possessing the records will be ordered to seal and eventually destroy them. Thus, if you want to have your records sealed, we suggest you complete that process before you ask the juvenile court to physically give you the records.

Fingerprint Note: As you've probably noticed, it's often necessary to provide your fingerprints when requesting copies of your record. Most police departments will take your prints so you can complete these applications, but will probably charge you a small fee (no more than $10; Penal Code §13300e).

D.   Correcting Errors on Your Criminal Record

LET'S SAY YOU'VE REVIEWED a copy of your state or local criminal record and you find a crucial error (i.e., your case was dismissed but your record makes no mention of it). Even though the law sets up safeguards to help prevent these types of errors, courts are still staffed with humans, and humans make mistakes. Records are frequently inaccurate, and may be especially so in your case if you've used more than one name, or your name is common.

If you do find an error, the laws regulating state and local records give you the chance to have it corrected.

1. California Criminal Records

If the error appears on your California Department of Justice criminal record, fill in the form entitled "Claim of Alleged Inaccuracy or Incompleteness," which appears in the Appendix of this book. On the form, you'll be asked to make a statement about what's wrong on your record and to provide evidence to show that there is, in fact, an error.

Normally, the best way to provide this information is to obtain copies of your court record showing a dismissal or other action that you wish to bring to the attention of the Department of Justice. Other times, the information you seek will be in the possession of the prosecuting attorney (usually the district attorney, but sometimes the city attorney) or the public defender.

Once you send in your claim form and your evidence of error, the Department will check it out, correct your record accordingly, and notify anybody who received a copy of the record in the previous 90 days of the correction.

If there's a dispute over whether an error has been made, you're entitled to a hearing to determine the truth of the matter (Penal Code §11126c). If you need a hearing, we suggest you contact a lawyer for more information.

Your claim form and any other information or correspondence should be sent to the Record Review Unit at P.O. Box 903417, Sacramento, CA 94203-4170.

2. Local Criminal Records

If the error appears on your local criminal record, you should contact the local agency and ask them for the form or procedure needed to correct your record. Once your request is received, the agency has 60 days to review your information and let you know the results of their investgation. If the agency agrees that an error was made, your local record will be corrected and anybody receiving a copy of it within the preceding two years will be notified of the change. If the agency disagrees that there was an error, then you're entitled to a hearing (Penal Code §13324c).

3. F.B.I. Records

The F.B.I. Identification isn't the source of the information on your record. The F.B.I. receives its information from the California Department of Justice. if you've been successful in correcting your California record, the Department should notify the F.B.I. to correct their record. However, you may also complain directly to the F.B.I. if you believe their record on you isn't accurate. You should direct your challenge to: Assistant Director of the F.B.I., Identification Division, Washington D.C. 20537. The F.B.I. will then forward the challenge to the state agency that submitted the data and request that they verify or correct the challenged entry. If the state agency responds with a correction, the F.B.I. should make changes on their record.

E. Criminal Matters on Credit Records

IN ADDITION TO CRIMINAL RECORDS kept by federal, state and local agencies, information about your criminal case may also appear on your credit record. When a case is filed in criminal court, that case file is a public record. Credit agencies examine public records of all types of court cases, and some will include criminal records.

There are time limits on how long different types of information can be kept on your credit record and if your case ended without your being convicted, then all reference to that case should be deleted immediately. If your case ended with a conviction, on the other hand, the conviction may remain on your credit record for no longer than seven years [Civil Code §1785.13(7) and 15 U.S.C. 1681(c)(5)]. For a complete discussion on how to get a copy of your credit record and make corrections if there are errors, see *Billpayers Rights,* Honigsberg & Warner, Nolo Press. Order information is found at the back of this book.

chapter 3 —————————————————

how to find your
record cleaning remedy

A. Introduction

FINDING THE RIGHT REMEDY to fit your record cleaning needs is almost like buying a new pair of shoes. Shoes come in many styles, colors and sizes. For each style you need to find the right size for your feet. You do this by trying them on and walking around, looking in a mirror, and checking where your toes are. In this chapter, we'll give you some preliminary information common to all the remedies and then help you choose the "do it yourself" chapter which covers the remedy best suited to your individual circumstances.

B. Some Preliminary Information

1. Who Can Help You?

The first big questions you need to decide up front are:
- Who's going to prepare your court papers?
- Is somebody going to represent you at the hearing?

To answer these questions, it's necessary to ask three more questions:
- Do you want to hire a lawyer?

- Do you want the probation department to prepare your court papers for you?
- Do you want to prepare your papers yourself?

a. Hiring a Lawyer

You may hire a lawyer to prepare all the forms and appear with you on the day of the hearing. This could cost as much as $500. Whether or not you end up having a lawyer do the whole thing, you might want a short consultation on some of the questions that might arise with respect to each of the remedies covered in the next eleven chapters. Other than a limited consultation, however, we believe that in most cases a lawyer is unnecessary and you can do it yourself. If you do hire a lawyer, be sure he or she is knowledgeable in the field. This usually means that the lawyer specializes in criminal law. Also, make sure you know what the lawyer will charge before you start.

b. Using the Public Defender's Office

In some counties, the public defender may be able or willing to help you for nothing if you are extremely low on funds. Don't count on it, however. Public defenders are generally too busy to give these kinds of issues the time they deserve.

c. Letting the Probation Department Do It

The easiest and cheapest way to clean up your record is to have the county probation department do it. Look in the section of the telephone book that has all the county agencies listed. You must do this in the county where your record was "earned," which may be different from where you now live. For example, if you now live in Los Angeles County, but had your encounter with the police or courts in San Francisco, you'll be dealing with the San Francisco Probation Department.

If there are separate listings for juvenile and adult probation matters, contact the appropriate division, depending on whether your case was handled in juvenile or adult court. Tell them you want their assistance to get your record sealed or expunged under the law authorizing your particular remedy. This information will be provided when you get into your particular "how to do it" chapter.

Some probation departments will prepare all your forms and get your record cleaned, although you may have to fill out a questionnaire and be interviewed as part of the process. However, most probation departments are facing problems caused by increasing caseloads and may be too busy to do this for you. Also, in many counties the probation department won't help you clean your records unless your probation was the "formal" or "supervised" variety (information

about probation is provided later in this chapter). At any rate, you may as well try probation first, but be ready to do it yourself if they won't help. If you were sent to a California Youth Authority facility and have a parole officer, your parole officer may do all the work to get the records for that case cleared.

d. Doing It Yourself

If you think you would like to do it yourself, or if no one will help you, we will provide specific step-by-step guidance on how to use the more common remedies. Don't let the thought of doing your own legal work scare you. Just be patient and follow our instructions carefully.

2. Photocopying Note

One of the great inventions of all time is the photocopy machine. Each of our remedies involves filling out several forms. Although we provide you with one copy of each necessary form in the Appendix, there are no spares. Before you start filling out a particular form, it would be a very good idea to make a couple of copies so you'll have extras to work with in case you make a mistake. It might be an extra hassle, but it's usually worth it. Copies can be cheaply and easily made at your local copy center.

3. Criminal Records from Other States

Although each of the remedies have specific limitations discussed in the appropriate chapter, all the remedies have one major limitation in common. None of them apply to convictions or arrests that occurred in another state or federal offenses handled in federal courts. Thus, for example, if you were convicted of burglary in Michigan or Florida, this book will not be of help to you. Remember, only California criminal or juvenile records are covered in this book.

4. Civil Suits Against Police

In many cases, persons who have had contacts with the police decide to bring civil suits to recover damages for the way the police treated them. If you have such a suit pending at the present time, or are thinking of suing the police, do not use any of these remedies without first checking with your lawyer.

5. A Little Jargon

Throughout the book we will be using the words "petition" and "application" to refer to the initial request to the court that something be done about your criminal record. Since the laws authorizing the remedies sometimes use "petition" and sometimes "application," we have tried to do the same in the various chapters. However, we may have slipped occasionally and used the wrong word. Don't worry. Whichever version you see, it still refers to that original document.

Also, in several of the chapters, we will be using the terms "expungement" and "dismissing your conviction" more or less interchangeably This is because the law itself talks about "dismissing your conviction," while people in the criminal justice "business" tend to refer to this process as expungement. We want you to become familiar with both phrases, but either will do fine. Technically, when your conviction is dismissed, you still have a record. Your record is not expunged or erased.

6. How We Provide Examples

Throughout the book, we give examples of how the proper form should be filled in. To do this, we have selected portions of the particular form and called them "boxes." The following is a portion of an application that we call Box 6 for reference purposes only.

EXAMPLE

2. I will be/was 38 years old on _____.

Often, the box will not correspond to the number (in this case, Number 2) in the form itself, as in the example shown above. If you just remember that the Box #s are all for the purpose of providing examples and do not refer to the number in the form itself, you can avoid confusion.

C. Some Preliminary Questions

AT THIS POINT WE'RE GOING to ask you nine questions to help you identify the correct remedy. If you have two different types of records, then you may want to use two remedies. For example, if you have a juvenile court record and were later arrested as an adult, you would want to pursue the remedies discussed in Chapters 4 and 10. Also, in some cases it's necessary to undertake one remedy before you can do another. For example, if you were convicted of a crime as an adult but want to go back and seal your juvenile records, you will probably want to use the remedy in Chapter 7 or 8 and then use the remedy in Chapter 4. In each of the chapters, we recommend other remedies that may also apply to your situation. To begin, however, use our suggestions in this chapter to decide which remedy to turn to first. If you answer "yes" to any of the questions below, turn to the chapter indicated.

Note: We've provided you with some information about each question to help you decide on your answer. If this isn't sufficient, a chart is provided at the end of this chapter. If you're still stumped, go to the chapter that looks the closest to your situation and start reading. At the beginning of each chapter we discuss the eligibility requirements for the remedy provided. With a little diligence, you'll find the remedy best suited to your particular record.

1. Did your case begin and end in juvenile court?

Juvenile court was set up to handle certain types of cases involving minors. If somebody under 18 commits a crime, they are said to be "delinquent." The crime is referred to as a "602 Offense" (named after the law that defines all offenses committed by a minor as "delinquent acts").

If the minor commits acts that aren't crimes as such, but that violate his or her status as a minor—such as being truant, refusing to obey a parent, or being out on the street late at night in the company of undesirable persons—they are said to be "status offenders" and their cases are referred to as "601 cases."

If a minor is neglected or mistreated in some way by his or her parents, he or she may be brought into juvenile court as a "dependency" case.

If you were under 16 when you had your scrape with the law, and ever appeared in court, then you have a juvenile court record. If your case involved "delinquency" (crime) or a "status offense" (i.e. truancy), you should turn to Chapter 4. If your court appearance had to do with "dependency," turn to Chapter 5.

If you were between 16 and 18, there's a possibility that your juvenile court case was transferred to adult court. If this happened and you were convicted of a misdemeanor in the adult court, turn to Chapter 11. If your case was transferred but you were not convicted of any offense (your defense was dismissed for one reason or another) turn to Chapter 12. If you don't know what you were convicted of, or even whether you were convicted, read on. The important point here is that if your case began and ended in juvenile court, then your remedies are found in Chapter 4 or 5. If your case was transferred to adult court, your remedies are most likely found in Chapters 11 and 12.

Two Important Notes: 1) If you don't know the answers to some of our questions, call the lawyer or probation officers who handled your case. You won't even have to talk to the lawyer or probation officer in many cases, since their staffs will frequently be able to provide the answers. 2) If your record was earned before March 7, 1973, your case may have remained in juvenile court if your offense or behavior occurred before you turned 21.

2. Did your record result from marijuana possession, or use of marijuana paraphernalia, or being in a place where marijuana was being used?

If your answer to this question is "yes," turn to Chapter 6 for a very nice surprise. This is one of the best remedies available.

Note: The remedy in Chapter 6 is for simple possession cases (as well as the paraphernalia and "being in a place" charges). If your conviction was for possessing marijuana for sale, or selling or growing it (cultivating), this remedy is not available. If you're not sure exactly what your record consists of, turn to Chapter 2 for an explanation of how to obtain a copy of it. Or, you might want to call your lawyer or probation officer, if you have one, and get the answer from either of them.

3. Were you convicted of a crime that involved being placed on probation?

If you were convicted of a crime, one of the following three events occurred:
- You entered a guilty plea in court. Pleading guilty always results in a conviction.
- You entered a "nolo contendere" or no contest plea. Pleading "no contest" always results in a conviction.
- You were found guilty by a judge or jury after trial. This event always results in a conviction.

There are procedures whereby guilty and no contest pleas can be withdrawn or set aside and convictions reversed or set aside on appeal, but if this happened in your case, you probably would have known about it.

Unless you have specific information to the contrary, if any of the above three events happened to you, you were convicted. Otherwise you were not.

If you were convicted of a crime (in adult court, remember) and your sentence involved any probation whatsoever, then turn to Chapter 7. This is your chapter whether your crime was a misdemeanor or a felony.

Probation is an alternative to serving your entire sentence in prison or jail. If you were put on probation, you may have spent some time in jail, but most of the jail or prison sentence would have been suspended so long as you lived up to your probation conditions.

There are two types of probation:

• "Supervised probation" is where you are assigned a probation officer to report to. This type of probation, sometimes called "formal" or "departmental probation," is most often imposed for felony and serious misdemeanor convictions.

• "Unsupervised probation" is where you are not told to contact anyone in the probation department. You still have to comply with your probation conditions but as long as you keep your nose clean during the probation period, you generally have no problems. This type of probation is often referred to as "court probation," "summary probation", or "informal probation."

If you were put on probation, you lived and worked where you wished as long as you obeyed the conditions, such as obeying all laws, paying restitution to the victim, and, in some cases, regularly contacting your probation officer. If any of this sounds familiar, you were probably on probation.

Here's the point: It's quite possible you were placed on probation and didn't really know it because you weren't assigned a probation officer. Nevertheless, if you were placed on any kind of probation at all, Chapter 7 is the remedy for you. If you just can't remember, contact your lawyer or the court clerk for further information about whether you were on probation.

4. Were you convicted of a misdemeanor only and not put on probation for any part of your sentence?

In order to answer this question, you'll have to know whether your conviction was for a misdemeanor or a felony. Most of you will already know the answer to this one. If you don't, the easiest way to find out is to call your lawyer and ask. If that doesn't work, however, find out whether the offense you were convicted of could have landed you in the state prison. If so, it was probably a felony. On the other hand, if your offense was only punishable by time in the county jail and/or a fine, then it was a misdemeanor.

Wobbler Note: Certain crimes can be considered as misdemeanors or felonies depending on how the district attorney wants to charge you. These crimes are called "wobblers" because they can "wobble" from a felony to a misdemeanor. The way you tell whether your offense was a wobbler is to find out whether the offense can be punished either by time in the state prison or by time in the county jail. If you were convicted of one of these, turn to Chapter 9 for a further discussion of what you can do to get a felony wobbler reduced to a misdemeanor wobbler.

Just for general guidance, felonies tend to be crimes like robbery, rape, murder, sale or possession for sale of any drug, and many federal offenses.

Crimes like disorderly conduct, trespass, possession of marijuana, petty theft (shoplifting), resisting arrest, being drunk in public, drunk driving, and illegal possession of a knife are usually misdemeanors.

If you don't know whether your crime was a felony or a misdemeanor and can't easily find out, you may want to do a bit of legal research. Again, we refer you to the Nolo Press book *Legal Research: How to Find and Understand the Law,* by Steve Elias, as an excellent reference tool.

If you were convicted of a misdemeanor and did not have probation as part of your sentence, turn to Chapter 8.

5. Were you arrested or detained but never convicted?

In order to have been arrested, you must have been taken into custody, at least for a little while *and* charged with a crime. Just being stopped by a policeman and questioned does not mean you were arrested. And even if you were taken into custody and later released because of insufficient evidence or for some other reason *without charges being filed against you,* your arrest will magically turn into a non-arrest, termed "a detention" (Penal Code §849.5).

If you are unsure whether you were arrested or detained, you may have to obtain a copy of your record to find out. To do this, read Chapter 2. If you were arrested or detained, you may be eligible to have the record destroyed if you can prove your factual innocence. To learn more about this remedy, turn to Chapter 10.

6. Did you ever receive an "honorable discharge" from the youthful offender parole board?

If so, turn to Chapter 13 for your remedy.

7. Do you qualify as a rehabilitated narcotics addict?

If so, turn to Chapter 14. If you don't know, turn to Chapter 14 anyway. You won't be told what to do, but you'll receive some valuable information about what has happened to your record.

Hopefully you'll have been able to answer a resounding "yes" to at least one of these questions. If not, turn to the chart on the next page and see whether this gives you a better perspective. If you still haven't a clue, start browsing through the chapters. Each chapter begins with some questions to make sure you qualify for that particular remedy.

In some of the chapters, after we go through the eligibility requirements and explain the advantages and disadvantages of completing the procedure, we will show you how to complete the procedure without a lawyer. We will explain who you should contact to get the paperwork done for you, or if you would rather do this work yourself, we'll take you through all the steps necessary to successfully complete the remedy.

In the other chapters, we will go through the eligibility requirements and explain what happens to your record after you complete the procedure, but we will not give you any instructions or forms. The reasons why we have done this are either:

1) the remedy is easy enough to do without all the detail; or
2) the remedy will be done by somebody else for you automatically; or
3) so few people are eligible for that particular remedy that we chose to save space. If you are one of those people, please accept our sincere apologies.

What happened to your case?	Your Chapter
• Did your case begin and end in juvenile court?	Chapter 4
• Was your case involved solely with dependency?	Chapter 5
• Did your case involve marijuana possession, paraphernalia, or "being in a place"?	Chapter 6
• Were you convicted of a felony or misdemeanor and placed on probation as part of your sentence?	Chapter 7
• Were you convicted of a misdemeanor and not placed on probation as part of your sentence?	Chapter 8
• Were you convicted of a felony that also could have been charged as a misdemeanor (wobbler)?	Chapter 9
• Were you arrested or detained, but not convicted of any crime, and are able to prove your innocence?	Chapter 10
• Did your case start in juvenile court but result in a misdemeanor conviction in adult court?	Chapter 11
• Did your case start in juvenile court but end in adult court without conviction?	Chapter 12
• Were you honorably discharged from CYA by the Youthful Offender Parole Board?	Chapter 13
• Do you qualify as a rehabilitated narcotics addict after treatment in a state institution?	Chapter 14

juvenile delinquency and status offense records

A. Introduction

IN THIS CHAPTER WE SHOW YOU how to clean your records for behavior that occurred when you were under the age of 18 (or under 21, if the behavior occurred prior to March 7, 1973). This remedy consists of two stages. The first one results in your records being sealed, and the second involves their actual physical destruction.

Fortunately, in addition to its other special "treatment" of juveniles, the juvenile court system also offers one of the most complete record "cleaning" remedies available. You're protected from having a black mark on your record for a mistake you may have made while you were "young and immature." However, if you want that black mark removed, you must take action. If you don't take the necessary steps, nothing happens, and your record won't be sealed.

B. Are You Eligible to Get Rid of Your Juvenile Record?

NOW IT'S TIME TO SEE if you're eligible to seal your juvenile records. Not everyone is. Like most other laws, the law we describe here has some exceptions and limitations. To determine your eligibility for this remedy, we've pretended we're traveling on a road with signs, which are actually questions specifically designed to help you assess your situation and determine whether to continue or take an exit. Also, there may be a detour to another chapter or a delay. Stay with us each step of the way and you'll be able to effectively wipe out your entire juvenile record.

1. Why were you detained?

The first road sign on our journey says, "This way for anybody detained as a juvenile for committing a crime." If the reason you got in trouble was that you were accused of committing a criminal act (called a "delinquent act" in juvenile court lingo), you're on the right road. Keep on traveling to the next sign.

If you were detained because you were a "status offender," i.e., you got in trouble because of your status as a minor for such as acts as truancy from school, disobeying your parents, or occurrences such as these, you should stay with us.

If you were taken into custody because you were a "dependent" child (your parents or guardian abused you or didn't care for you properly and the court was asked to do something about it), keep reading for now. Later, however, we'll be asking you to exit to Chapter 5 for a slightly different form than the one we'll be using in this chapter.

2.   How did your case end?

The second traffic sign on our trip says: "Only people whose case went no further than juvenile court should proceed."

If you were under 16 when your record was "earned," then your case ended in juvenile court and you're entitled to remain on the trip.

On the other hand, if you were over sixteen *and* the court decided you weren't fit for juvenile court treatment, *and* your case was transferred to regular adult criminal court, you have a problem. Unless *both* of the following two statements are true, you'll have to detour and use one of the remedies described in Chapters 11 to 13:

- Your adult criminal court case ended without your being convicted; *and*
- You haven't been convicted in an adult criminal court on any other offense.

Are both these statements true as applied to you? If so, you're still on the journey (Welfare & Institutions Code §707.4). If not, turn to Chapters 11, 12 or 13.

Federal Court Note: If for some reason your case was handled in a federal court because your offense involved a federal crime, exit.

Let's summarize just to make sure we're on the same track. Whether you were detained without a court appearance, or had to appear in juvenile court, you're still on the road so long as your case wasn't transferred to adult criminal court. Even if it was, you can still remain with us if you weren't convicted on that or any other charge.

3.   Did the case end with a juvenile court finding that you committed a serious offense?

Our third traffic sign says "Pull over and wait if your juvenile court case ended with a finding that you committed any of the offenses listed in

Welfare & Institutions Code §707b." This section lists the most serious crimes of violence (murder, armed robbery, assault with a firearm, etc.) as well as certain sex, drug and weapons crimes. If your case ended with a finding that you committed one of these crimes, you must wait three years from the date the crime was committed before the court will order your juvenile court records sealed.

4.   Have you been in trouble since your juvenile matter ended?

Just about a mile along the way, a roadblock appears out of nowhere. The highway patrol pulls us over and asks the following questions:

- "Have you been convicted of a crime since your juvenile record occurred?"
- "Do you have a criminal case currently in the courts?"
- "Have you done something bad that might lead to a conviction in the future?"

If you can answer "no" to the above questions, you're entitled to pass the roadblock, get in the express lane and put it on cruise control. You've got it made. Skip the next several paragraphs and turn directly to Section C of this chapter. That's where we'll tell you a little more about your record and how to get rid of it.

If you had to answer "yes" to any of these questions, or even feel the need to hem and haw a bit, keep reading. You may still be able to complete our journey instead of detouring to another chapter.

5.   Do you understand the effect of a conviction after your juvenile offense?

There are three types of convictions that concern us here:

- Felonies
- Misdemeanors involving moral turpitude
- Regular misdemeanors and infractions

a. Felonies

If you were convicted of a pure felony (i.e., an offense for which you can be sentenced to state prison but not to the county jail) *after* you "earned" your juvenile record, it's time to part company, since later felonies disqualify you from getting your juvenile records sealed.

However, if you were later convicted of an offense that could have been charged as a misdemeanor *or* a felony (called "wobblers," remember?), see Chapter 3, Section C(4), and turn to Chapter 9 for suggestions on how to get the offense reduced to a misdemeanor if it was treated as a felony in your case. If you do this, you may be able to rejoin us. Also, if you get your felony conviction dismissed using the procedure described in Chapter 7, some judges may then allow you to seal your juvenile records. Check with your lawyer or probation officer to find out the policy of the juvenile court judge in your county.

b. Misdemeanors Involving Moral Turpitude

If your trouble led to being convicted for a misdemeanor considered to be a "moral turpitude" crime, it's also time for the exit sign, since a conviction for a "moral turpitude" crime *after* your juvenile record was "earned" disqualifies you for this remedy.

What is a moral turpitude crime? Good question. If we translate that phrase into simple English, it means crimes that reflect poorly on your morals, such as fraud, theft, sex and drug related crimes. If your misdemeanor falls within these or similar topics, ask a lawyer if the crime you were convicted of is a "moral turpitude" crime.

If you get your moral turpitude misdemeanor conviction dismissed using the procedure described in Chapter 7 or 8, some judges will then allow you to seal your juvenile records. Check with your lawyer or probation officer to see how things are done in your county.

Shoplifter's Note: Even though shoplifting seems to be a minor crime, it may qualify as a moral turpitude crime because of the theft involved. Again, check with your lawyer.

c. Regular Misdemeanors, Infractions, and Pending Cases

If you've been convicted of a misdemeanor, infraction, or have a case pending against you, and still want to seal your juvenile record that was earned before these subsequent events, all isn't lost. In order to seal your juvenile records, the court must conclude that you've been rehabilitated since the time your juvenile record was earned. Obviously, later convictions reflect poorly on your "rehabilitated status." It all depends on what the convictions were for, when they occurred, or what you're charged with. A minor traffic ticket (infraction) won't have the same devastating impact as would a conviction for criminal trespass, for example.

If you've had some trouble since your juvenile record days and don't know whether a court would now consider you rehabilitated, check with your lawyer or the juvenile probation officer for your county and tell him or her your situation. You may be able to proceed now or you may have to wait for awhile. In any event, if your later scrape with the law didn't involve a felony or moral turpitude misdemeanor, then sooner or later you may be able to seal your juvenile record.

If your juvenile record was for "dependency," then, likewise, you may be able to seal your record after awhile, even if you've had a subsequent conviction. To do so, however, you'll need to detour to Chapter 5.

Summary

If you've been convicted of a felony or a misdemeanor involving moral turpitude since your juvenile record was earned, take the next exit. But remember that you may be able to have the later conviction dismissed by using the remedy in

Chapter 7 and/or Chapter 9. If you've been in other trouble with the law, check with a probation officer to see whether you're rehabilitated, and if not, how long you must wait to seal your juvenile records. If you've been in no trouble since your juvenile record was earned, you probably qualify to have your records sealed.

If you're still with us, your juvenile case wasn't serious enough to be transferred to criminal court and you have a relatively clean record since your juvenile case ended.

6. Are You Over 18?

The last question is simple. Are you over 18? If you are, great, you qualify. If you're under 18, you need to wait until your eighteenth birthday, or until five years after your case was closed. This would only affect you if your record was earned before your thirteenth birthday, and would more likely occur in "dependency" cases.

C. Roadmap Review

We've just traveled the road leading to the sealing and destruction of your juvenile records. When some people take trips into the unknown, they like to see where they're going and where they've been. If you're one of these, take a look at the map that follows.

If your record involves "dependency" (see Section B, Question 1 of this chapter), now is the time to detour to Chapter 5.

D. Practical Results of Record Sealing

LIKE MAGIC, WHEN YOUR RECORD is sealed, whatever is contained in it is considered never to have happened. It's like rewriting history. If you're ever asked to tell about your juvenile record, you're specifically entitled to say, "Record? I have no record." Great. You can even deny ever having your record sealed. But as long as your records remain "unsealed," the police may continue to disclose information about your juvenile court matter to any other police department or agency that has a "legitimate" need for the information. If you're convicted of a crime, the judge may consider all unsealed juvenile records to increase your sentence or deny you probation (Welfare & Institutions Code §828, Penal Code §1203b). If you're in prison, the Board of Prison Terms may review unsealed juvenile court records to evaluate if you should be released (Welfare & Institutions Code §829).

Unfortunately, there's some bad news. This record sealing device isn't perfect—there are a few exceptions. In other words, history is rewritten for most purposes, but not for all.

Insurance companies are permitted by the Department of Motor Vehicles to delve into your sealed records for the purpose of determining your rates. If you're asked about your record by an insurance company for purposes of automobile insurance, tell all. However, they should only be interested in automobile related violations.

If the record you had sealed was from a case where the juvenile court determined you committed a crime labeled as a felony, it's possible[1] that your record may be used against you if you're later charged with a crime. One part of the Victim's Bill of Rights (Proposition 8) entitles adult criminal courts to use juvenile records involving felony convictions to increase punishment and discredit your testimony if you're later charged with a crime.

Review Chapter 1, Section A, Question 6 for a few more exceptions.

Other than these exceptions, getting your record sealed will give you a brand new start.

E. How to Get Your Records Sealed

IF YOU'VE BEEN TO COURT before, you may have had your fill of it. Between the papers, the attorneys, the judges, the clerks, the bailiff, the reporter, and the language, you may very understandably be ready to pounce on anybody who even mentions the word "court." In fact, many people who are eligible to seal their records don't ever do it for exactly this reason—they want never to have anything to do with court again.

If you're one of those people, stop reading, take a deep breath, and think about whether you want to proceed, since, unfortunately, getting your records sealed involves at least some contact

---

[1]The validity of this law, implemented as part of the Victim's Bill of Rights (Proposition 8, June 1982) has not been reviewed by the Supreme Court at the present time (January 1989). However, it does conflict with another law which considers all juvenile court matters to be civil and not criminal in nature (Welfare & Institutions Code §203); and court of appeals decisions have concluded that juvenile court adjudications may not be used to increase penalties. *People v. West* (1984) 154 Cal. App. [3d] 100 and *In Re Anthony R* (1984) 154 Cal. App. [3d] 772 (confirmed).

As to whether juvenile court adjudications may be used to discredit testimony of a witness, one appellate court decision said it could not [*People v. Sanchez* (1985) 170 Cal. App. [3d] 216].

with the court. The contact should be relatively painless, however.

To get your juvenile records sealed, you must prepare a form called a "petition" and file it with the juvenile court clerk. The clerk sends copies to the probation department and the district attorney's office. Upon receiving the copy, the probation department in most counties will prepare a report for the court to let it know if you're eligible to have your records sealed. Your criminal record will be checked to make sure you haven't been convicted of any felony or moral turpitude crimes and that you've been rehabilitated. As part of this process, the probation department may want to interview you.

A court hearing date will be selected when you file your petition. If the probation report declares that you're eligible, the judge will probably order your records sealed at the hearing. Copies of that Order will then be sent to the different agencies who have a copy of your record. Upon receiving the Order, the agencies will be obligated to seal your record, or send them to the juvenile court clerk, who'll destroy them. If you need a review of who might help you out with the procedure, go back and reread Chapter 3, Part B(1).

F. Which Court Forms to Use

SOME COUNTIES HAVE THEIR OWN printed form petitions to seal juvenile records. These only require you to fill in the blanks, sign at the bottom, and send them in. If such a form exists in your county, you'll be able to find it through 1) the juvenile court clerk; 2) the probation department section that handles juvenile court matters; or 3) the public defender's office. If such forms exist for the county where your case occurred, we strongly recommend you use them. If not, use the ones we provide.

ELIGIBILITY MAP
TO SEAL JUVENILE RECORDS

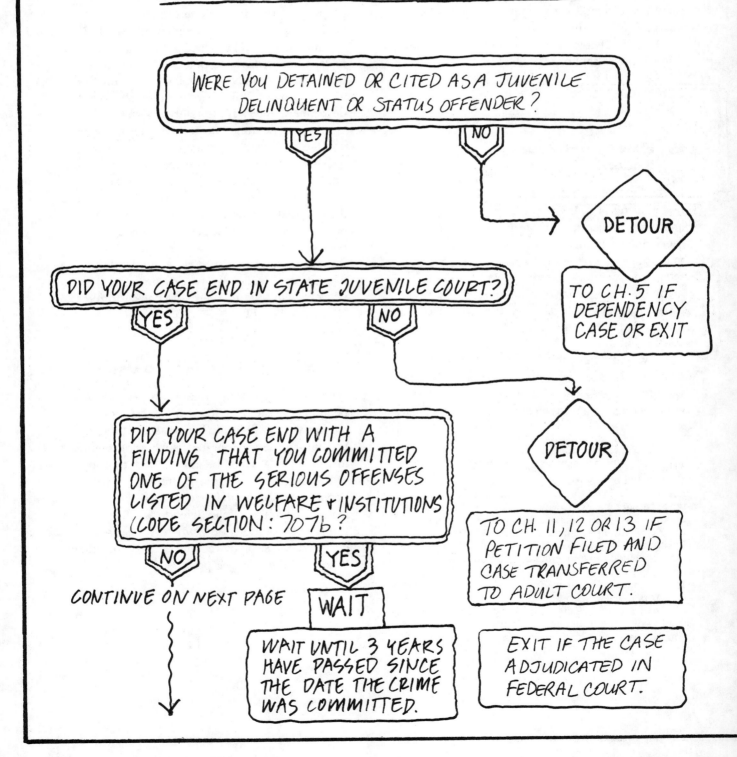

WERE YOU DETAINED OR CITED AS A JUVENILE DELINQUENT OR STATUS OFFENDER?

YES

NO

DETOUR

TO CH.5 IF DEPENDENCY CASE OR EXIT

DID YOUR CASE END IN STATE JUVENILE COURT?

YES

NO

DID YOUR CASE END WITH A FINDING THAT YOU COMMITTED ONE OF THE SERIOUS OFFENSES LISTED IN WELFARE & INSTITUTIONS (CODE SECTION: 707b?

DETOUR

TO CH. 11, 12 OR 13 IF PETITION FILED AND CASE TRANSFERRED TO ADULT COURT.

NO

YES

CONTINUE ON NEXT PAGE

WAIT

WAIT UNTIL 3 YEARS HAVE PASSED SINCE THE DATE THE CRIME WAS COMMITTED.

EXIT IF THE CASE ADJUDICATED IN FEDERAL COURT.

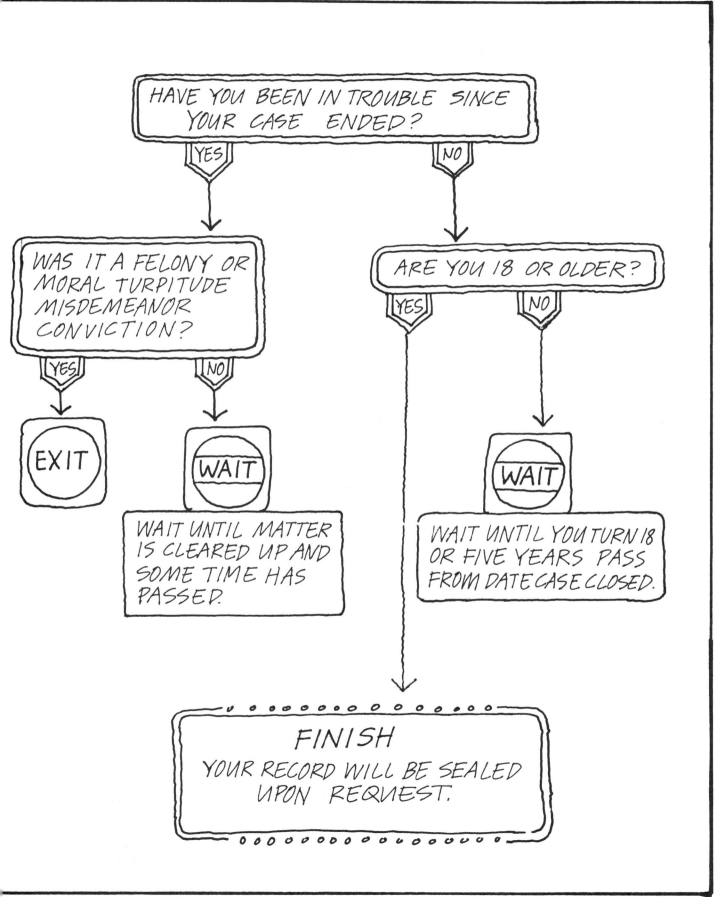

Remember, if you had more than one juvenile case, you'll need a separate petition for each case. If cases occurred in different counties, you must file your petition in the county where the case occurred, so you may be dealing with more than one county. Sometimes, if the crime was committed in one county, but the juvenile lives in another county, the case is transferred to the county where the juvenile lives. If this happened in your case, you'll need to file petitions in both counties.

If your county doesn't have printed forms, we've drawn up a petition that is representative of official forms used in some counties and that should be acceptable to the court. Turn to the Appendix and locate the blank form entitled "Petition for the Sealing of Juvenile Records (Welfare & Institutions Code §781)." Make sure you have the correct one and then tear it out (carefully). Don't fill it in until you've carefully read through this section, where we use a story to demonstrate how each part should be handled. After you're through with the examples, you'll then be prepared to put you own information in.

THE SAD STORY OF JULES DEVLIN YOUNG

On a warm summer evening in 1976, Jules Young, who was sixteen at the time, and a few friends were drinking beer and having a good time. The combination of the beer, the warm weather and the company led to an incident Jules would regret. At the urging of his friends, Jules climbed through the window of his neighbor's garage and "borrowed" the neighbor's motor bike. Jules and his friends rode the bike in a park in the neighborhood. When the neighbor returned home and found his motor bike missing, he called the police. A police car on patrol near the park saw Jules and his friends riding the missing bike. All of them were arrested. Since Jules was 16, a petition was filed in juvenile court charging him with burglary (a felony if committed by an adult).

At juvenile court, Jules agreed to admit to committing the crime of trespass (a misdemeanor if committed by an adult) and was put on probation under court supervision for one year. Jules wants to seal his records involved with this case and has decided to use our form.

Step 1: Fill Out Petition

FILL IN BOX 1

ATTORNEY OR PARTY WITHOUT ATTORNEY (NAME AND ADDRESS)	TELEPHONE NO
JULES YOUNG 60 ROLLING HILLS ROAD KENSINGTON, CA 94706	(415) 526-4151
ATTORNEY FOR (NAME) PETITIONER JULES YOUNG, in pro per	

Box Number 1 is for your name, current address and telephone number. In Jules' case, his address is 60 Rolling Hills Road, Kensington CA 94706 and his phone number is (415) 526-4141.

Since Jules is representing himself, as you'll be doing, we've put "Petitioner Jules Young, In Pro Per" (which is Latin for representing himself).

FILL IN BOX 2

SUPERIOR   **COURT OF CALIFORNIA, COUNTY OF** ALAMEDA
SITTING AS THE JUVENILE COURT
STREET ADDRESS   400 BROADWAY
MAILING ADDRESS   same
CITY AND ZIP CODE   OAKLAND, CA 94607
BRANCH NAME   JUVENILE COURT WEST

Box Number 2 contains the information about the court that you're asking to seal your records. In our little story, since Jules originally went to the juvenile court in Alameda County, we put Alameda after "County of" and put in the address of the juvenile court, which is located at 400 Broadway, Oakland CA 94607. In Alameda County, there are two branches of the juvenile court. In this case, Jules will be filing his petition in the west branch.

To find out the proper mailing address and branch of your court, look in your phone book under the name of your county, locate the entry for the juvenile court division of the superior court, give them a call, and find out the court address and branch. If there's no entry for the juvenile court, just ask the superior court clerk. If the mailing address is different than the street address (such as a P.O. Box), fill both addresses in.

FILL IN BOX 3

In the Matter of
JULES DEVLIN YOUNG   Date of Birth: 6-2-60

Box Number 3 contains the title of the case and your birthdate. In the case of Jules Young, we put his name right after the "In the matter of." In your case, you would put your name. This box also calls for a birthdate. Jules was born on June

2, 1960. When were you born? Remember not to make a very common mistake and put the current year for the year of your birth. You weren't "born yesterday."

FILL IN BOX 4

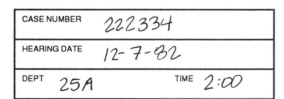

CASE NUMBER	222334	
HEARING DATE	12-7-82	
DEPT 25A	TIME	2:00

Box 4 asks for a lot of information that you don't have yet. Therefore, we won't be filling most of it out at this time. One item you should know about, however, and that is your case number, if you had one. If a petition was filed against you in

the juvenile court, a case number will have been assigned to your case and stamped on any court papers you received. If you still have any of these, dig them up, find the number and put it in the case number section. If you disposed of such mementos of your court experience, call your attorney or probation officer, if you had one, and ask either of them. If this doesn't work, call the juvenile court clerk's office.

If no petition was ever filed, you never had a case number. In such a case, make sure you tell this to the clerk when you go to file your papers (more about that later).

In Jules' case, his juvenile court case number was 222334, and that's the number we've provided in this example.

When you file your petition with the court clerk, you'll receive a hearing date, time, and the department of the court in which your hearing will be held. In Jules' case, when he took his papers to court, his hearing was set for 12/7/82 at 2:00 p.m. in Department 25A.

FILL IN BOX 5

```
Petitioner, the undersigned, declares:
1.    ☒ I am now at least 18 years old.
      ☐ 5 years or more have passed since the termination of Juvenile Court
        jurisdiction, which occurred on or about _____.
```

This box calls for one of two choices. Almost all of you'll be checking the first box. Since Jules was over 18, he did also. If you're under 18, either wait until you're over 18 or until five years have passed since you were completely finished

with your juvenile court case. This means if you were put on probation, you'd have to wait until five years after your probation expired. As we mentioned, most of you're over 18, right?

FILL IN BOX 6

```
2. I will be/was 38 years old on  JUNE 2, 1998        .
```

This box asks when you'll be 38. Strange question? You bet. If your record was "earned" for committing a crime (delinquent act), your court records cannot be destroyed until you turn 38. Records of other agencies, such as the probation department, may in fact be destroyed

at an earlier time for convenience sake. The information in this box will tell the court when your records should be destroyed. Just think, though, if you're 21 in 1984, you'll be 38 in 2001. Wonder what life will be like then? In Jules' case, he'll be 38 in 1998.

FILL IN BOX 7

```
3. Yes  No    Part or all of this case involves violations of misdemeanor
   ☐    ☒     or infraction traffic laws.
```

This is the box that most of you'll be checking "no." If your offense involved a traffic offense, however, you'll be checking "yes," and your county may require you to pay a filing fee. In Jules' case, he never admitted to any traffic violations and they were therefore not a part of

the case. Some counties may require filing fees even if there was no traffic offense. Call the juvenile court clerk to find out if there are any fees. If you cannot afford the fee, the court may have an application form to get the fees waived.

FILL IN BOX 8

> 4.   I have not been convicted of any felonies or of any misdemeanors involving
>   moral turpitude and rehabilitation has been attained.

You don't have to check anything in this box, but at the bottom of the petition you'll be signing under penalty of perjury that this statement is correct. If you don't know the answer, check with your former lawyer and probation officer for advice. Also, refer back to Section 3 of this chapter and Chapter 3 for the meaning of these terms.

FILL IN BOX 9

> 5.   I am informed and believe, and on that information and belief allege, that
>   the following law enforcement agencies and public offices have custody of
>   records, including records of arrest or detention, relating to this case:
>
>   ☒ a. Clerk, Juvenile Court, in this county
>   ☒ b. Probation Department in this county
>   ☒ c. District Attorney's office in this county
>   ☒ d. Public Defender's office in this county
>   ☒ e. California Bureau of Criminal Identification, Department of Justice
>   ☒ f. Federal Bureau of Investigation
>   ☒ g. The following law enforcement agencies:
>   *ALBANY POLICE DEPARTMENT*
>   ☐ h. Department of Motor Vehicles
>   ☐ i. Others on attached list

Are you still with us? Good. Now, pay close attention. This one is important. The reason you're sealing your records is to make sure you have a totally clean slate. As we've pointed out, records are slippery characters that may pop up in any number of agencies. Especially in this age of computers, it's easy for agencies to routinely collect records on everybody.

In this part of the petition you'll be listing the agencies that should be notified to seal your records. In Jules' case, he remembered the following agencies may have had his record and accordingly checked off the appropriate boxes. These were:

☐ Box "a," which names the juvenile court clerk in Alameda County;

☐ Box "b," which names the probation department in Alameda County;

☐ Box "c," which names the district attorney's office in Alameda County;

☐ Box "d," which names the public defender's office in Alameda County;

☐ Box "e," which names the California Bureau of Criminal Identification;

☐ Box "f," which names the F.B.I.;

☐ Box "g," which specifies the police department originally responsible for detaining (arresting) Jules;

Special Note on Boxes "g" and "i": In our example, Jules had a simple case and didn't need to list a whole bunch of law enforcement agencies under box "g" or other agencies on an attached list under box "i." However, your case might be different.

Box "g" is your opportunity to list any criminal law enforcement agencies that might have your record. As you can see, there isn't any room on the form unless you're going to list one or two of these agencies at most. If you need more room, check box "g," say "see attached page," take a clean 8-1/2" by 11" sheet of white paper, label it Attachment "5g" at the top and either type or print the name of any of the following agencies that you remember coming in contact with in connection with your juvenile record:

City Police Department (as in Jules' case)
Highway Patrol
County Sheriff's Office
Park Rangers
Fish and Game Wardens
Town Constable or Marshall
U.S. Drug Enforcement Agency (DEA)
U.S.Customs (for any offense involving the
  national borders;
Immigration and Nationalization Services (INS)

If the adjudication in juvenile court required you to register with local law enforcement agencies as required by Penal Code §290, be sure to list all law enforcement agencies that you've registered with, so all of them will be ordered to destroy your registration records. In most cases, these juvenile records will automatically be destroyed when you're 25 years old (Penal Code §290d4).

Box "i" gives you an opportunity to list additional agencies or entities that might have a copy of your record. Using the same procedure as for box "g," list any of the following agencies that may have a copy of your record on a separate page labeled attachment "5i."

Any school you attended during your juvenile court involvement if one of your probation conditions involved attending school; or if the superintendent and certain school personnel were given copies of juvenile court records pertaining to certain drug and violent crimes (Welfare & Institutions Code §827b);

Any laboratory that may have been involved in testing drugs if your record was drug related;

Any rehabilitation center with which you may have become involved in connection with your juvenile record (like halfway houses, drug rehabilitation centers, etc.);

The welfare department if your parent(s) were receiving public assistance when your brush with the law occurred;

Any juvenile detention center in which you were placed for any length of time.

We've asked a great deal of you in this section. Just remembering all the possible contacts associated with your record may have kicked up bad memories.

Sorry about that. Still, it's very important to root out your record wherever it may be and fix it once and for all. It's like fumigating a house. If you miss just a few fleas, cockroaches, or spiders, the little monsters will find a way to re-create an entire empire. We're sure you know what we mean.

So, if you sort of glossed over this section, take a breather and then go back to make sure you did the best job possible. It may be helpful to contact your former probation officer or lawyer to get their ideas about which agencies and entities might have your record.

FILL IN BOX 10

> WHEREFORE, petitioner prays for an order that all records, papers, and exhibits in this case in the custody of the Juvenile Court, including the Juvenile Court record, minute book entries, and entries on dockets, and other records relating to the case in the custody of such other agencies and officials named in this petition be sealed; that a copy of the order be sent to each agency and official named in this petition ordering such agency and official to seal the records in its custody and to destroy the sealed records
> ☐ in 5 years or
> ☒ when I am 38 years old,
> and that the proceedings in this case shall be deemed never to have occurred.

This section is called the "prayer," aptly enough, and is very much like the real thing where you ask to be forgiven for your "sins." The only choice to be made in this paragraph is to inform the court when your sealed records should be destroyed. In Jules' case, his record involved a criminal act (excuse us, a "delinquent act" in juvenile courtspeak), and therefore his records cannot be destroyed until he turns 38. If your record was for a "status offense" (remember, an offense against your status as a minor), then you can have it destroyed five years after sealing and you would check the first box. For most of you, the second box, which Jules checked, will be the right one.

FILL IN BOX 11

> I declare under penalty of perjury under the laws of the State of California that the foregoing is true and correct.
>
> DATED: SEPTEMBER 22, 1982 _____ Jules D. Young _____
>   (PETITIONER)

This is the place where you sign under penalty of perjury that everything you've said earlier is true. Pretty heavy, but don't let it scare you. As long as you did your best to be accurate, there will be no problem. Nobody is going to do anything to you for an honest mistake—honest. Also in this box, put the date you sign the petition.

Well, that's it as far as the petition goes. You should now take the form that you detached from the Appendix ["Petition for the Sealing of Juvenile Records" (Welfare & Institutions Code §781)] and fill in your own information as we've suggested in this section. Take your time and there should be no problems, but first read the following Photocopy Note. If you were referred here from Chapter 5 (dependency case), you'll be looking for the form referring to Welfare & Institutions Code §389. Since both of these petitions look very similar, it's very important to double check and make sure you're using the right one.

Photocopy Note: One of the great inventions of all time is the photocopy machine. Before you start filling out the form it might be a good idea to make a couple of spares so in case you make a mistake, you'll have additional copies.

Step 2: Fill Out Order Sealing Juvenile Records

"What's this," you may be groaning, "another form? Ugh!" Afraid so, but it's not as complicated as the first one. Here's the situation. The petition will get you your hearing, and if everything is in order, the judge will order your records sealed and eventually destroyed. However, unless there's a form called an "order" for the judge to sign, his words will disappear into thin air.

In some counties the court will prepare the order on the day of the hearing. Check with the court clerk by phone to see whether you need to prepare the form or whether the court will do it for you.

Note: If you used a printed form petition provided by your county, the order may be at the bottom of the form. If it is, you can ignore this step.

If you have to prepare the order for the judge to sign, we've provided you with the form itself. It's located in the Appendix and is labelled Order Sealing Juvenile Records (Welfare & Institutions Code §781). If you were referred here from Chapter 5, look for the Order Sealing Juvenile Records with the reference to Welfare & Institutions Code §389. Tear the correct form out and look at it as we take you through the following instructions (don't forget to make a couple of spare copies). Ready? Here goes.

The top part of the form should look familiar. It's exactly the same layout as your petition and you should put exactly the same information.

What next? Now, look at your form. There are four sections (1 through 4). Don't fill in any information in the first three sections. The juvenile court clerk will fill these sections in on the day of your hearing (more about the hearing later).

Now take a look at the boxes next to each agency listed in Number 4. Look familiar? They should. They were on your petition (Box 9). Now, take a look at your completed petition. Check the same boxes here that you checked on your petition. If you made additional lists of agencies or entities and attached them to your petition, do exactly the same here. As a matter of fact, you can photocopy your lists attached to your petition and attach the copies to the order.

After you've taken care of this part of Section 4, go on to the next part (Part b). Which box did you check in Box 10 of the petition? Whatever you did there, do the same here and fill in the date of your thirty-eighth birthday if you checked the second box.

You should check box before 4c only if you were required to register by Penal Code §290 as a result of this juvenile court case. Getting your juvenile court records sealed will end this registration requirement and all agencies holding registration information will be required to destroy it. Most juvenile court cases don't require registration, so most of you should leave the box blank.

Now, take a good look at Part d. This is your reward for your efforts. Need we say more? Well, Yes, one more word: Don't sign or date the order. That's for the judge to do.

Step 3: Make Copies

You'll need three copies of the completed petition. You'll need more of the order, however. Count the number of boxes you checked in Section 4 of the order (the agencies and entities) and the number of agencies and entities listed on any attachments. Add them all together, add one more, and make that number of copies. Why so many? Well, when the judge signs the order sealing your record, these copies will each be stamped with the judge's name and mailed to the agencies and entities listed in your order. This is how they know to seal and eventually destroy your records or to mail them to the juvenile court clerk for destruction.

Step 4: File Petition and Obtain Court Hearing Date

Now that you've filled out your petition and order and made the correct number of copies, it's time for a trip to the juvenile court. While it's possible to do this filing by mail, there's a much greater chance that something confusing will happen. We recommend you take care of this in person if possible.

No matter how good a job you did on your papers, actually taking them to the juvenile court can be a bit scary. After all, this will be the first time somebody will be looking to see if you goofed. Please believe us when we say, don't worry. Court clerks are usually quite helpful and if you've done something wrong, they'll make suggestions about how to correct your error. If you followed our instructions, however, this probably won't be necessary.

To file the papers, find the juvenile court clerk handling matters for the court where your case was filed and/or heard. Usually, they will be in a separate location from other superior court clerks. It might be wise to use the phone first to find exactly where they are located. You should also find out if there's a filing fee (so you'll know how much money to bring with you), whether a set of fingerprints are required (they are in some counties), and if you need to bring the prepared order with you at that time.

Anyway, when you find the right clerk hand him or her the original and 3 copies of your petition. These will be for filing. The juvenile court clerk is required to send one copy of your petition to the district attorney and another copy

to the probation department. The third copy will be stamped and returned to you.

Tell the clerk you want a hearing date on your petition and be prepared to offer several dates convenient to you. When you agree on a date, you'll also learn the time of the hearing and the department in which it will be held. Either the clerk will tell you to fill in this information yourself (remember, in Box 4 of the petition we left this blank), or, they'll fill it in for you. You'll definitely have to fill this information in on your own copy, which you'll keep for your own records. The clerk will then "file stamp" the original and copies, and will allow you to file stamp your copy. This is proof that you filed the papers. What does "file stamp" mean? If you look at your petition in the upper right hand corner, you'll see the following box:

This is where the clerk will stamp the original and copies for court filing and where you'll stamp your copy.

After this ritual is over, you should ask the clerk whether you can "lodge" the "Order Sealing Your Record" in the court file so it will be available at the hearing. The Clerk will either say "fine" or tell you to bring them to the hearing or bring them back before the hearing at some future date. When you lodge papers, you're not filing them, but simply placing them in the court file. There's no particular advantage to lodging them as opposed to bringing them with you to the hearing, but see the following note.

Note: In some counties you may not have to appear at the hearing if the probation department's report is favorable and it recommends that your records be sealed. If this is the case, make sure you get your orders to the clerk some time before the hearing. In these situations, the judge will review your petition, the probation department's report, and sign the order without anyone being present in court to discuss your petition.

Step 5: Attend Court Hearing

Attend the hearing if you have to, or want to. It's usually a good idea. Enjoy the fruits of your labors first hand. At the hearing, the judge will decide whether to order your juvenile record sealed. The judge will review your petition, the probation department's report and recommendation, and make sure that the district attorney was sent a copy of your petition by the clerk. If everything is in order and you're eligible, the judge will sign the order.

If you're required to attend the hearing, the judge may ask you a few brief questions to make sure you're eligible. However, if you followed our roadmap without any problems, you have nothing to worry about. If your petition is denied, contact a lawyer.

If your records are ordered sealed, the clerk will send the extra copies of the order to all the agencies you listed. Once the agencies report back to the court that they've obeyed the order and sealed your records or mailed them back to the court clerk, your records are sealed. Congratulations! Whatever happened is now considered "never to have occurred" and those sealed records will eventually be destroyed. Good luck.

chapter 5

your juvenile dependency record

WELCOME TO THOSE OF YOU who got here directly from Chapter 3 or detoured from Chapter 4. The remedy discussed in this chapter only applies to juvenile court records arising from juvenile dependency cases, i.e., cases where your parents or guardian were accused of not caring for you properly or mistreating you in some way, or where you were considered to be a danger to the public because of a mental or physical disorder (Welfare & Institutions Code §300).

This remedy allows you to seal your "dependency" record and have it destroyed five years later. There is no particular benefit to having your dependency record sealed or destroyed since you were not accused of doing anything wrong. Nevertheless, it is possible that somebody in the future might confuse your "dependency" record with a "delinquency" or "status offense" record and hold it against you in some way. If this prospect worries you, then read on. We'll tell you how to get rid of your dependency record.

Step 1

Turn to the Appendix and locate the form entitled "Petition For Sealing of Juvenile Records" (Welfare & Institutions Code §389). Tear it out.

Step 2

Now, turn back to Chapter 4, Section E, "Which Court Forms to Use." While referring to the form you took from the Appendix, read the instructions for Steps 1-5. Since this is a special remedy, however, you won't have exactly the same choices presented to you in Chapter 4.

Specifically, in Chapter 4, you're asked to choose whether your records will be destroyed in five years or on your thirty-eighth birthday. The form used for the remedy for dependency records doesn't provide a choice, since this remedy automatically involves destruction after five years, no matter what your age. For the purposes of filling out the other parts of the form, and the procedures to be followed for preparing the order for the judge to sign, the instructions are the same.

The general advice we offer on copying your documents, filing them with the court, and obtaining a court hearing, is the same for Chapters 4 and 5. For all practical purposes, there is no difference between the Chapter 4 remedy and this one. Since there are different legal authorities for the two remedies, however, we've provided a separate chapter for each.

chapter 6 ——————————————————

marijuana records

A. Introduction

IF YOU WERE EVER BUSTED for possession of marijuana, or some of the crimes incident to possession, such as having "paraphernalia" or "being in a place where marijuana was being used," we have some great news for you.

If your bust occurred after 1976, your records will be automatically destroyed two years later. You don't have to do anything. Read the next section (Section B) for more information about how this should happen and whether you qualify.

Even if your bust occurred before 1976, however, you're still entitled to have your records destroyed. It won't happen automatically, however. You'll have to file an application. For complete instructions on how to do this, turn directly to Section C.

B. Destruction of Post-1976 Marijuana Bust Records

THE CRIMINAL RECORDS for your case will automatically be destroyed by the court and each agency having a copy of your record if you were either arrested or convicted in 1976 or later for:

Possession of marijuana in any amount
OR
Giving away less than 28.5 grams of marijuana
OR
Transporting less than 28.5 grams of marijuana

All you have to do is satisfy the terms of your sentence (i.e., pay the fine, complete probation, etc.) and wait two years.[1] Then all of the records of your marijuana case will magically disappear like a puff of smoke.

If you're ever asked whether you've been arrested or convicted, you'll be able to answer "no," assuming this is your only conviction and arrest, of course.

You may have wondered how this "automatic" remedy works. When you're charged with these certain marijuana offenses, a special sticker or notation should be put on your file that says "Marijuana purge—Upon closing or 2 years from *date* this record is to be purged pursuant to Health & Safety §11361.5c" (the Health & Safety Code section responsible for this remedy).

Sometimes there's a large gap between having to do something and actually doing it. This is especially true for agencies. To make sure your records have actually been disposed of, we

---

[1]If you were under the age of 18 and are charged with possession of less than 28.5 grams of marijuana at a school, your records will not automatically be destroyed until you are 18 years old.

recommend that after the two-year period you double check by requesting a copy of your record and seeing what turns up. Nothing should, but if one or more of the agencies hasn't done what they should have, remind them, citing the proper code section (Health & Safety Code §11361.5c). Chapter 2 tells you how to get a copy of your record.

Important Note: Only marijuana offenses are covered by this remedy and only certain ones at that. For example, the law doesn't apply to possession of marijuana for sale, growing marijuana, or selling marijuana. These offenses are still considered serious crimes.

C. Getting Rid of Your Pre-1976 Marijuana Record

IF YOU GOT CAUGHT before 1976, back in the time when marijuana cases were treated more seriously, you can still get your records destroyed by filling out an application form and sending it, with a fee, to the California Department of Justice. Only the following types of offenses are covered by this record destruction law, however:

- Possession of marijuana (but not for sale);
- Possession of paraphernalia used for smoking marijuana;
- Being present in a place where marijuana is being used;
- Being under the influence of marijuana.

Note: If you pleaded guilty to maintaining a place for the use or sale of narcotics as part of a plea bargain when your case started out as a possession of marijuana charge, you can also use this remedy, according to a recent court decision.[2]

If your marijuana related offense falls within any one of these five charges, you can apply to have these old records destroyed by completing the application shown in the next section.

D. Applying to Get Your Pre-1976 Marijuana Record Wiped Out

THE CALIFORNIA DEPARTMENT of Justice has prepared an application form for you to fill out if you want your pre-1976 marijuana records destroyed. The form is titled "Application to Destroy Arrest/Conviction Records [Health & Safety Code §11361.5(b)]" and is located in the Appendix. Tear it out now for reference during the following discussion. However, we suggest waiting to fill it out until after you're through reading. Also, make a couple of photocopies before you begin. You should also be able to find these forms in any police or sheriff's department and can obtain them directly from the Department of Justice. If you take a look at the form on the next page, you'll see that it's easy to fill out.

Note: If you aren't eligible for this remedy, you may be eligible for one of the others in the book. Turn back to Chapter 3(C) for a further analysis of your situation.

Let's run through an example of how this procedure works. All names and dates are purely fictitious and all puns are intended.

---

[2]*Hooper v. Deukmejian* (1981) 122 Cal. App. [3d] 987.

HEALTH AND SAFETY CODE SECTION 11361.5(b) STATES IN PART:

"The department may request, but not require, the applicant to include a self-administered fingerprint upon the application. If the department is unable to sufficiently identify the applicant for purposes of this subdivision without such fingerprint or without additional fingerprints, it shall so notify the applicant and shall request the applicant to submit such fingerprints as may be required to effect identification, including a complete set if necessary, or, alternatively, to abandon the application and request a refund of all or a portion of the fee submitted with the application as provided in this section. If the applicant fails or refuses to submit fingerprints in accordance with the department's request within such reasonable time as shall be established by the department, or if the applicant requests a refund of the fee, the department shall promptly mail a refund to the applicant at the address specified in the application or at such other address as may be specified by the applicant. However, if the department has notified the applicant that election to abandon the application will result in forfeiture of a specified amount which is a portion of the fee, the department may retain such portion of the fee as the department may determine will defray the actual costs of processing the application, provided the amount of such portion retained shall not exceed ten dollars ($10.00)."

The Department of Justice has determined that upon notification an applicant shall submit fingerprints within 15 days of such notification. If the applicant does not respond to the notification within 15 days, or chooses not to submit fingerprints and abandons further pursuit of the application, the applicant will forfeit $10.00 to the department to defray processing costs. The remaining fee will be refunded.

THE FOLLOWING INFORMATION IS OPTIONAL. COMPLETION WILL EXPEDITE THE PROCESSING OF YOUR APPLICATION.

SELF-ADMINISTERED
RIGHT INDEX FINGERPRINT:

DATE OF ARREST	ARRESTING AGENCY

Social Security No.: _____ Driver's License No.: _____

FOR DEPARTMENTAL USE ONLY

Certificate of Compliance

☐ No record located for this application.

☐ The application has been fully complied with as of this date.

_____ _____
Signature   Date

AGENCY NOTIFICATION:

1. _____

2. _____

3. _____

4. _____

STATE OF CALIFORNIA

BUREAU OF IDENTIFICATION

Department of Justice

2601 C STREET

TO APPLICANT:

Health and Safety Code (H&S) Section 11361.5(b) states that if prior to January 1, 1976 you have a record of conviction(s) and/or an arrest(s) not followed by conviction for violations of H&S 11357, 11364, 11365, 11550 or their predecessors, you may apply to the Department of Justice for destruction of record(s) in connection with these offenses. If you meet the requirements for arrest record destruction, complete the following application.

APPLICATION TO DESTROY ARREST/CONVICTION RECORDS
(Health and Safety Code Section 11361.5(b))

TYPE OR PRINT THE FOLLOWING INFORMATION:

Applicant:	Last Name	First	Middle
	Bogart,	Mary	Jane

Also Known As:	Last Name	First	Middle
	Roach	Mary	Jane

Address:	Number	Street		Apt. No.
	19	Green St		

	City	State		Zip Code
	Grass Valley	CA		95945

Telephone:	Business		Residence
			(916) 273 - 1991

Date of Birth:	Month	Day	Year
	9 - 19 - 55		

Signature:	Mary Jane Bogart	Date	10-29-86

Mail this application with a fee of $37.50 (in the form of a U.S. Money Order, certified check or cashier's check made payable to the Department of Justice) to:

Department of Justice
Bureau of Identification
P.O. Box 903417
Sacramento, California 94203-4170

IMPORTANT: See reverse side for additional information pertaining to Health and Safety Code Section 11361.5(b) and optional information.

THE SAD STORY OF MARY JANE ROACH

Our story starts in Grass Valley (where else?), California. (Yes, there really is a Grass Valley.) Our young friend is named Mary Jane Roach. Back in 1975, she was at a party that got a little too noisy for the neighbors. The police were called. As they approached the house, they got a strong whiff of marijuana. The party was interrupted and Mary Jane was among those unfortunate enough to get busted. She was charged with possession (plastic baggie containing a green leafy vegetable-type substance found in her purse), paraphernalia (water pipe on the table), and being present in a place where marijuana was being used. How her case ended isn't important. It could have been dismissed or she could have been convicted. The only important point here is she was arrested and/or convicted of *only* those marijuana offenses listed in Section C. Since she was, and she got caught *before* 1976, she can apply to get her records destroyed.

Mary Jane is now ready to fill out the application. She's married to Hubert Bogart and is now known as Mary Jane Bogart. She'll fill in her current name in the top box and put her former name (the one she used when she was arrested) in the second box. She fills in all the other information on the front page of the application form, signs it, gets a money order for $37.50, makes a copy for her records, and sends it to the Department of Justice. Pretty simple so far, right?

If all goes well, she should get her application form back with the bottom of the back page filled out by the Department of Justice showing that her application has been fully complied with and that the police department that arrested her, the court where the charges were filed, and any other agencies applicable to her case have been notified to destroy their records on her case.

If the Department of Justice replies it cannot locate her records, she can either:

Fill in the optional information on the back of her application, such as the date of arrest, arresting agency, right index finger print, social security and driver's license numbers, and send it back to the Department of Justice. Hopefully this will do it;

OR

Ignore the request for this additional information and forget about getting her records destroyed, assuming they exist. By giving additional information to the Department of Justice to help them find your record, they may be getting data on you that they don't currently have. You should consider whether the benefit of getting your record found and destroyed under these circumstances is worth it. Everybody has different feelings about these things, and you'll have to make your own judgment. In the computer age, these questions are becoming extremely complex.

If Mary Jane decides to fill in the optional information, she should make her decision and get it off in the mail within 15 days of the date the application was sent back to her. Otherwise, the Department of Justice will conclude her failure to reply means that she doesn't want her records destroyed.

When filling in the optional information on the back, the arresting agency is the name of the police or sheriff's department which made the arrest. You can get your fingerprint put on your application by stopping in at most police departments and asking them to put your print on the application. They'll probably charge a fee for this service (unlike the other time they took your prints).

E. When Your Record Is Destroyed?

GETTING YOUR CRIMINAL RECORD destroyed is the most complete form of "record cleaning" available. If the only "stain" on your entire criminal record is this or other similar marijuana cases, your entire record will be physically destroyed. If there are other non-marijuana matters on your record, your record will be prepared again so that there's no notation about any of your marijuana cases.

Once your records are found by the Department of Justice, the F.B.I., the police department that arrested you, the Department of Motor Vehicles (if you were convicted), and the Probation Department (if you were on probation) will all be notified so that they can similarly destroy your records.

Regardless of what's supposed to happen, sometimes agencies don't take papers out of their filing cabinets or entries out of their computers when they're supposed to. After several months have passed, we recommend you obtain copies of your criminal records, as we suggest in Chapter 2, to see whether the agencies have complied. If they haven't, point this out to them and hopefully you'll get some action. All agencies have procedures to respond to requests for corrections of mistakes in their records.

Not only are your records destroyed under this law, but you also gain other important benefits if one more hurdle has been cleared. Two years must have passed since your arrest and/or conviction:

If you're asked about a prior criminal record on any type of application, you're authorized to say "no," so long as only the marijuana cases were on your record, of course. (Health & Safety Code §11361.7c).

You cannot be denied any form of professional license, permit or franchise by any state, county, or city department, board, or other agency because of your marijuana record. (Health & Safety Code §11361.7b). If you're a teacher, your school board may not fire you because of your marijuana possession conviction.[3]

If you're ever convicted of another crime, the judge may not consider your former marijuana conviction when sentencing you.[4]

If your old marijuana possession conviction was a felony, you may own or possess a firearm without the possibility of being prosecuted in the California state court system as an ex-felon in possession of a firearm. However, you might be in trouble with the feds.[5]

If you were required to register with the police department as a narcotics offender, that duty is ended.

Immigration Note: If you aren't a citizen, your immigration status may conceivably be affected by your conviction even though the record of it is destroyed. If any problem comes up, see an immigration specialist.[6]

Conclusion

THE DAY HASN'T YET ARRIVED when marijuana is totally legal, but some steps have certainly been taken in this direction. While the law may have exacted harsh penalties from you for your possession and use of marijuana, you now can at least remove the stigma and get a fresh start. For those of you whose brush with the marijuana laws has happened more recently, your life isn't over. You'll be able to accomplish what you wish without having the millstone of a criminal record tied around your neck. Good luck.

---

[3] *Governing Board of Rialto v. Mann* (1977) 18 Cal. [3d] 819.
[4] *People v. Flores* (1979) 92 Cal. App. [3d] 461.

---

[5] *People v. Boyd* (1979) 24 Cal. [3d] 285.
[6] *Matter of Moeller* (1976), 16 I & N, p. 65.

chapter 7

criminal convictions with probation

A. Introduction

MANY OF YOU WILL BE INTERESTED in this chapter. Under the law, persons with many types of criminal convictions are entitled to go back to court after a while and get their convictions dismissed. When this happens, the law says you're "released from all penalties and disabilities" resulting from the offense "except as otherwise provided by law." As we'll describe a little later, the "as otherwise provided by law" phrase makes this remedy less desirable than it might seem. Still, for most of you, the benefits of getting your prior conviction dismissed will probably outweigh the trouble involved.

The remedy discussed in this chapter is commonly referred to as "expungement." Technically, your record isn't "expunged." It's merely changed, with an additional entry that your conviction is dismissed. Many persons in the criminal justice system continue to refer to this procedure as "expunging" your record. We'll describe who's eligible to use it and what the benefits (and lack of benefits) are so you can decide whether expunging your record is worthwhile. If you decide to go ahead, we'll take you through the process step-by-step.

B. Are You Eligible to Have Your Conviction Dismissed?

NOT EVERYONE WITH A CONVICTION is eligible to use the remedy described in this chapter. Like most other laws, there are some exceptions and limitations. We'll go over the eligibility requirements by pretending we're on a road trip reading road signs. If you follow these signs, which are really questions, and are still with us on the end of the trip, you'll be eligible for this remedy. In some cases, you'll have to exit or detour to another chapter, or delay your remedy for awhile. At the very end of the chapter, we'll provide you with a map summarizing our trip. Let us proceed to the signs, or questions, which will help you make your determination.

1. Were you an adult when you committed your crime?

The legal age of adulthood is 18 or older unless your offense was committed before March 3, 1973, in which case it was 21 or older. If you weren't an adult on the date of the crime for which you were convicted, detour to Chapter 4, which discusses the remedy for getting rid of juvenile records. (If you were referred here from Chapter 11, forget this first requirement.)

Fitness Note: If you were a minor when your crime was committed and your case was transferred from juvenile to adult court because you were found *unfit* for treatment by the juvenile court, detour to Chapters 11 through 13.

If you answered "yes" to our first question, the light is green to continue your trip to the next.

2. Was your conviction in a California adult criminal court?

If it was, go on to the next question. However, if your case was in a juvenile court, detour to Chapter 4.

3. Did your case end with a misdemeanor or felony conviction?

Your case must have ended with you being *convicted* of at least one felony or misdemeanor crime. Remember, you were convicted of a crime if you:

- entered a "guilty" plea;
- entered a "no contest" plea (nolo contendere);
- were found guilty of a misdemeanor or felony by a judge or jury after trial.

If you weren't convicted of a misdemeanor or felony, but only an infraction, like a traffic offense, it's time for you to exit. If you aren't sure how your crime was classified, return to Chapter 3 for a discussion of these terms, or ask your attorney or probation officer if you had one. If your conviction was for possessing marijuana, detour to Chapter 6 for a very effective remedy.

Arrest Note: If you were arrested as an adult, but not convicted, *and* you believe you can prove your innocence, detour to Chapter 10 for a possible remedy.

If you were convicted of a misdemeanor or felony, however, and are still with us, let's go to the next question.

4. Were you convicted of failing to obey a traffic officer?

For some reason, the crimes of failing to obey a traffic officer (Vehicle Code §§2800, 2800.1, 2801, or 2803) aren't covered by this remedy. If your record isn't for these crimes, then continue to the next question.

5. Did your sentence involve probation?

In Chapter 3, we described probation as having to meet certain conditions in order to avoid serving all your sentence in jail. We also pointed out that probation may be either supervised or unsupervised. If you didn't have a probation officer to report to, you still may have been on court or summary probation and would qualify for this remedy. If you don't know what your status was, check with the court clerk. If your sentence involved probation, then you're still on the freeway and can continue to the next question. If your sentence didn't involve probation, and your conviction was for a felony, you'll have to exit unless your felony was a wobbler. For further information about wobblers, see Chapter 3, Section C(4). If it was a wobbler, then you can apply to have it changed to a misdemeanor (see Chapter 9), and then detour to Chapter 8.

Parole Note: Don't confuse probation with *parole*. Parole involves supervision by a parole officer, and involves many more restrictions than does probation. If you're uncertain whether you were on probation or parole, call your former lawyer, if you had one. Also, call the person to whom you had to report and ask him or her what your status was.

If you were convicted of a misdemeanor, and your sentence didn't include probation, detour to Chapter 8.

6. Are you off probation now?

In most cases, you cannot apply for the remedy set out in this chapter until your probation has ended. Your probation would have ended either when the period of probation imposed on you expired, or, if you were discharged from probation on an earlier date. If you're on probation now, however, and still want to get your conviction dismissed without waiting further, contact your probation officer or your attorney. Sometimes the "interests of justice" will permit you to use this remedy even if you're still on probation.

7. Did you successfully fulfill the conditions of your probation?

Being eligible to get your conviction dismissed is one of the rewards for doing well and performing all the conditions of your probation. For example, if you were required to pay restitution, or participate in a drug rehabilitation program, or to faithfully report to your probation officer, you must have done so in order to use this remedy. If there's evidence that you didn't successfully complete your probation conditions, then this remedy may be denied you.[1]

If your probation was revoked because you didn't perform your conditions of probation, but you were later reinstated and continued on to a successful completion of all conditions, you may be able to use this remedy in some counties. Check with your probation officer or attorney to find out about this. However, if your probation was revoked and you weren't reinstated, you're definitely not eligible.

Sometimes people are convicted of offenses while on probation but their probation is still not

---

[1] *People v. Turner* (1961) 193 Cal. App. [2d] 243.

revoked. If this happened to you, you should check with your probation officer or lawyer regarding your eligibility for this remedy.

8. Are you in criminal trouble now?

This last sign is more like a roadblock. You've been flagged over and are being asked some rather intimidating questions:
- Are you currently serving a sentence for any other offense?
- Are you currently on probation for another offense?
- Are you facing charges for any other offense?

If you can answer "no" to these questions, get in the express lane. Skip the rest of this section and go directly to Section C.

If you had to answer "yes" to any of these questions, or even felt the need to hem and haw a bit, keep reading. You may be able to complete our journey after a short delay.

If you're serving a sentence or are on probation for another conviction, you'll need to wait until your sentence and/or your probation ends for this other conviction before you can apply to dismiss your case from the earlier conviction.

If you're facing criminal charges on a new case that's still pending (you have been accused of committing a crime and you'll be going to court on those charges), you must wait until the outcome of that case has been determined. If that case ends with all charges being dismissed, you can immediately proceed with this remedy. If your new case ends in a conviction, then you must wait until your sentence and/or probation ends before proceeding further.

Quick Check: If you answered "yes" to Questions 1-7 and answered "no" to all questions asked under Question 8, you're eligible to get your conviction dismissed. If you want to double check the route we've been over, take a look at the map that follows.

In the next section, we'll take a look at the effects of getting your conviction dismissed, and then go on to getting the job done—assuming you decide it's worthwhile.

C. The Practical Effects of Getting Your Conviction Dismissed

AS WE MENTIONED, this law sounds great. We also pointed out, however, that it isn't all that it could be. First, let's look at the positive results of this remedy, and then, the negative ones.

1. Positive Results of Getting Your Conviction Dismissed

When your conviction is dismissed, your conviction cannot be brought up in a later trial involving civil matters (Evidence Code §788c). This may not seem like such a big deal, but if you later want a jury to believe your testimony in a case involving a car accident, or a business deal, and the other side is prevented from raising your criminal conviction to cast doubt on your credibility as a witness, you'll be very glad you dismissed your conviction. This would be of the greatest benefit if your offense was a felony and was for a moral turpitude crime (a crime reflecting on your morals and honesty, such as theft or rape). To read more about moral turpitude, turn to Chapter 4, Part B, subsection (5) and Chapter 1, Part B, subsection (1).

Another important benefit would occur if you're a non-citizen. Getting your conviction for a moral turpitude crime dismissed may prevent you from being deported.

Beyond these definite benefits, there may be numerous other situations involving private employment, employment with the federal government, and even public employment outside of California, where your dismissed conviction will stand you in good stead. It all depends on the requirements of the agency or business involved. If you apply for a job in federal or private employment, you can state you have never been convicted (but see "2. What Getting a Conviction Dismissed Won't Accomplish," below).

2. What Getting a Conviction Dismissed Won't Accomplish

Even if you get your conviction dismissed, it will *not* be of any benefit to you in the following situations:

• If your offense involved a major traffic offense, such as drunk or reckless driving, your record will continue to affect your eligibility for a driver's license under the rules established by the legislature and the Department of Motor Vehicles. So, if you were convicted of drunk driving, getting your conviction dismissed will have no effect on your losing your license if you get convicted again for this offense during the ensuing seven years.

• If you're convicted of another criminal offense in the future, your punishment may be increased and you may even be charged with a more serious offense, just as if you had never had your conviction dismissed.

• If you apply for a job with a California or local agency (in California), or a professional license, and the job application asks about criminal convictions, you must mention your conviction, even though it's been dismissed. However, you're entitled to call the dismissal to the attention of the agency, and this may well have a beneficial impact on your chances for the job.

The law doesn't cover how you should answer criminal conviction questions on applications for private or federal employment. Especially in regard to private employment, you should be able to answer that you've never been convicted of a crime if the dismissed case is your only conviction. However, an employer might be able to discharge you if your former conviction is later discovered, since the law doesn't speak to this issue one way or the other.

Getting your conviction dismissed doesn't change your status under the gun laws. Both state and federal laws prohibit ex-felons from possessing concealable firearms, and getting your conviction dismissed will have no effect on your right to possess guns.[2]

- If you've been convicted of a felony sex offense that requires you to register, your duty to register will continue (Penal Code §290.1) even after your conviction is dismissed.

Even though your conviction is dismissed, you may still be denied a professional license by California regulatory boards (Business & Professions Code §490). Licenses are often required for occupations, as in the case of lawyers, electricians, and optometrists. Although the fact that your conviction has been dismissed may operate in your favor when you apply for your license, the licensing board in question is still legally able to deny you your license if your conviction can be considered to be related to your ability to engage in the occupation in question.

The release from penalties and disabilities under California isn't recognized in many circumstances under federal law.

D. How to Dismiss Your Conviction

TO GET YOUR CONVICTION DISMISSED, you have to ask the court. You make your request by preparing a form called an "application," or in some cases a "petition," and filing it with the court clerk. A copy of the application must be sent by you to the probation department and the district attorney's office (in some areas it will go to the city attorney instead of the district attorney).

Upon receiving the copy, the probation department, in most counties, will prepare a report for the court to let them know if you're eligible to get your case dismissed. They'll check your criminal record to make sure you aren't serving a sentence and aren't on probation, or charged with another criminal offense. For the other remedies, they'll check to make sure you met the eligibility requirement for that remedy. As

---

[2]*Dickerson v. New Banner Institute, Inc.* (1983) 460 U.S. 103.

part of this process, the probation department may want to interview you. In some counties, you'll be charged a fee for this service.

In most counties, when you file your court papers a hearing will either be set at that time, or at a later time if the probation department hasn't yet completed its report. If the report declares you eligible to get your conviction dismissed, the judge will probably dismiss your conviction without further ado. In some counties, once your eligibility is determined, your case will be dismissed without a hearing. If you need a review of who might help you with the procedures, go back and reread Chapter 3, Part B(1).

E. Which Court Forms to Use

SOME COUNTIES HAVE THEIR OWN printed form petitions that only require you to fill in the blanks, sign at the bottom, and send them in. If such form petitions exist in your county (the county where your conviction occurred), you'll be able to find them at either 1) the criminal court clerk or 2) the probation department section that handles adult criminal court matters. Also, you might try the public defender's office. Some courts require you to use their forms, if they exist. Even if you don't have to, it's a good idea.

If there's no such form for your county, however, we've provided a form that's representative of the ones in use. Since our instructions apply to our own form, they may not be exactly what you need for the county form, but they should prove helpful. So, whether you use our form or the county's form, keep reading.

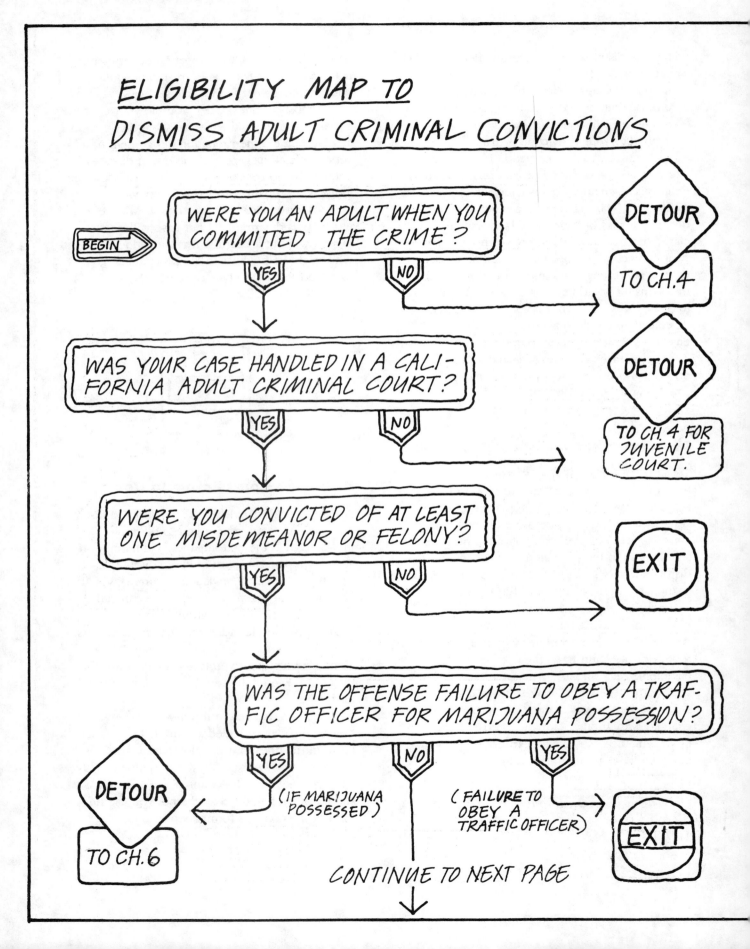

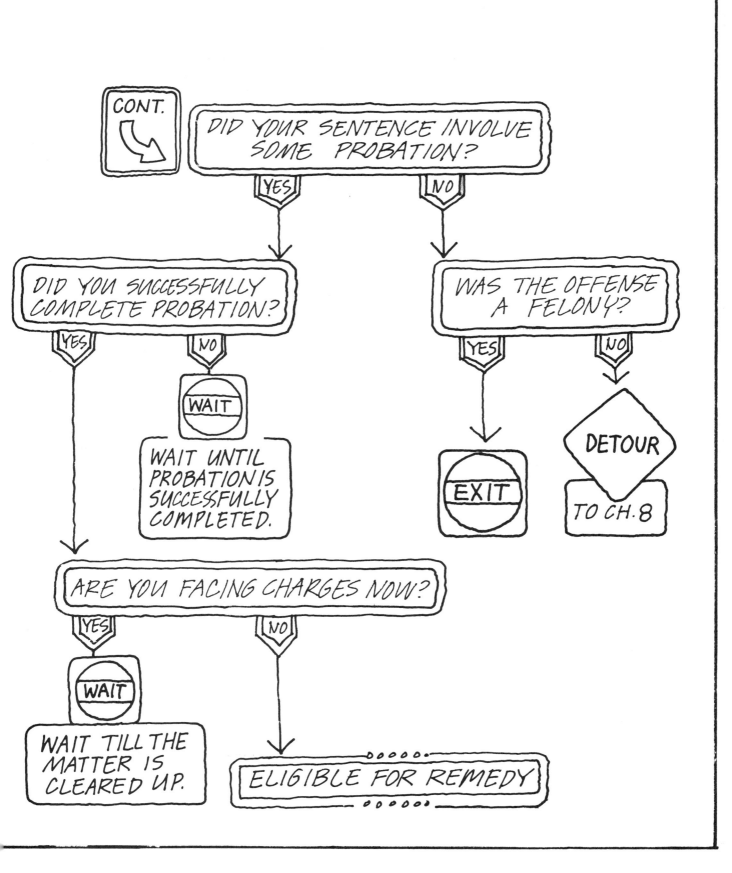

While some of the language may seem like Greek, it actually asks for very little information. We'll tell you how to fill it in. Turn to the Appendix and find a blank copy of the form included for your use ("Application to Withdraw Conviction, To Dismiss the Case, and for Relief from All Penalties and Disabilities Resulting from Offense —Penal Code §1203.4"). Make sure you have the right form before tearing it out. We recommend you not fill it in until you've carefully read this section. However, if you want to do both at the same time, don't forget to photocopy the form first, just in case.

To help you understand our instructions, we've prepared a little story.

THE SAD STORY OF MIKE "STICKY FINGERS" JAEGGER

Mike "Sticky Fingers" Jaegger wanted to acquire a portable tape recorder with earphones. He was never able to save enough money to buy one. A friend bragged how easy it was to just "take" the unit from a stereo store in the neighborhood. Mike tried to duplicate his friend's method of ripping off a portable recorder, but was caught by store security guards. A criminal complaint was filed, charging Mike with petty theft. After a few court appearances, Mike pleaded guilty to trespass (Penal Code §602L). He was put on probation for 18 months and was required to report to a probation officer every month, participate in a community clean up program for 10 hours, pay a fine of $100.00, and conform to other standard probation conditions. Now Mike wants to have his conviction dismissed.

Step 1: Prepare Application

Now we're going to take the facts from the story and fill in the form, part by part. As an example, each part is numbered, so when we say "Fill in Box 1," for instance, you'll know what we're referring to. After you've read through this section, you'll be writing in your own facts on the form you removed from the Appendix.

FILL IN BOX 1

ATTORNEY OR PARTY WITHOUT ATTORNEY (NAME AND ADDRESS)	TELEPHONE NO
MIKE JAEGGER 2120 MICHIGAN AVE. MOUNTAIN VIEW, CA 94379	(415) 966-6181
ATTORNEY FOR (NAME) *DEFENDANT MIKE JAEGGER, in pro per*	

Box 1 is for your name, current address and telephone number. In the case of Mike Jaegger, his address is 2120 Michigan Ave., Mountain View, California, and his phone number is (415) 966-6181.

Since Mike is representing himself, as you'll be doing, we've put him as "Defendant in pro per," which is Latin for "representing yourself."

FILL IN BOX 2

```
COURT OF CALIFORNIA, COUNTY OF SANTA CLARA
          PALO ALTO - MOUNTAIN VIEW JUDICIAL DISTRICT
STREET ADDRESS
MAILING ADDRESS   270 GRANT AVENUE
CITY AND ZIP CODE  PALO ALTO, CA  94306
BRANCH NAME
```

Box 2 contains the information about the court you're asking to dismiss your conviction. In our little story, Mike's conviction occurred in the Santa Clara County Municipal Court, Palo Alto-Mountain View Judicial District. If your conviction was for a misdemeanor, it was probably handled in municipal court. In most large counties, there are several municipal court judicial districts. If you don't know which one was involved in your case, call the court clerk and ask. Most districts include the names of the cities that are covered. Also, you might find this information on any court papers you may have kept. Finally, you can call your former probation officer or attorney. If your conviction occurred many years ago, it's a good idea to call to make sure the court hasn't moved or been consolidated. Once you find out, fill in the word "municipal" before "Court," the name of the county after "County of," and the

name of the judicial district before the words "judicial district" on the second line.

If your conviction was for a felony, it occurred in superior court. Superior courts aren't divided into districts, but large counties may have different *branches*. Find out what branch your superior court was, and put it in after the words "Branch Name." Put the name of the county where your conviction occurred after "County of," and write the word "Superior" before the word "Court." Don't fill in anything on the second line before the words "judicial district."

This box also requires the address of the court. You can often find this in the phone book, or it may be on your old papers. The court clerk will also tell you over the phone. Make sure you get the correct address. If the mailing address is different than the street address (such as a P.O. Box), fill both addresses in.

FILL IN BOX 3

```
THE PEOPLE OF THE STATE OF CALIFORNIA
                 vs.
       MIKE JAEGGER
                        Defendant
```

This box contains the title of your case. Put your name after the "vs." If you go by more than one name, make sure you put the name your

conviction occurred under. Otherwise, the court may get confused and problems may develop.

FILL IN BOX 4

CASE NUMBER	*19196*
HEARING DATE	
DEPT TIME	

    This box contains several items. The case number should be the same as it was on the case that resulted in your conviction. If you no longer remember, or don't have court papers that contain it, call your probation officer, attorney, or the court clerk to get it.

    The rest of the box should be left blank at this time. Later on, when you get a hearing date, these items will be filled in.

FILL IN BOX 5

    2. On *MARCH 3, 1980* , I was convicted of the following offense(s):
        Penal Code Sec. 602L – Trespass

    Here, you need to put the date of your conviction and the actual offense for which you were convicted. In Mike's case, he learned from his probation papers that his conviction occurred on March 3, 1980, and that he was convicted for the crime of "trespass" (Penal Code §602L). If he didn't have any papers, he could have obtained this information from his probation officer, his lawyer, or the court clerk.

    Remember: The crime(s) you were convicted of may be different from the ones you were originally charged with. Your guilty plea may have been the result of a "plea bargain," where the original charges may have been reduced to a less serious offense. If your case went to trial, a jury or judge may have found you guilty of crimes different from those you were originally charged with.

FILL IN BOX 6

    3. As a result of that conviction, I was put on probation for a time period of ___*1*___ years ___*6*___ months.

    This box calls for information about your period of probation. In Mike's case, this was for eighteen months, or one year and six months.

FILL IN BOX 7

    4. ☒   My period of probation ended on *Sept. 3, 1981* .
        ☐   I was discharged from probation, prior to the termination of my probation period, by an order of this court, on _____.
        ☐   I request that I be granted the relief available under Penal Code §1203.4, even though my probation has not ended, in the interests of justice, because of the following reasons:

This box requires you to indicate when your probation ended. In Mike's case, his probation ended automatically eighteen months after it was imposed. This is true in most cases. Also, the petition gives you the opportunity to ask that your conviction be dismissed even though you're still on probation. See Section B(6) of this chapter for a further discussion of this possibility. Check only one of these three choices.

Items 5-8 on the petition don't call for a response. However, when you later sign the petition, you'll in effect be agreeing that each of these statements is true. If you stayed with us on our road trip in Section B, then you'll be able to agree with these statements.

```
5.  During the entire period I was on probation, I fulfilled all
    of the conditions of probation.

6.  I am not now serving a sentence for any other criminal offense.

7.  I am not now on probation for any other criminal offense.

8.  I am not now charged with the commission of any offense in
    any pending criminal case.
```

FILL IN BOX 8

```
WHEREFORE, applicant moves that:

1.  ☒   The court allow me to withdraw my plea of guilty/nolo contendere and to
        enter a plea of not guilty;
    ☐   The court set aside and vacate the jury's verdict or the court's finding
        of guilty after the trial of the above-entitled action;

2.  The court dismiss this action pursuant to Penal Code §1203.4.

3.  The court order that I be released from all penalties and disabilities
    resulting from the conviction(s) except as otherwise expressly provided by
    law.
```

This box is known as the "prayer," and is very much like the real thing. It informs the court of what you want, and asks that you be forgiven for your acts. In Mike's case, he entered a guilty plea and therefore checked the first box. Most convictions result from guilty or no contest pleas, and the chances are pretty good that you, too, will be checking the first box.

However, if your conviction resulted from a guilty verdict after trial by judge or jury, you'll want to check the second box. Check only one of these two boxes.

FILL IN BOX 9

```
    I declare under penalty of perjury under the laws of the State of California
that the foregoing is true and correct.

DATED:  September 17, 1981 _____  Mike Daczy_____
                                        DEFENDANT
```

In this box, you put the date you're filling out the application and sign under penalty of perjury. This means that to the best of your knowledge, every statement that you made, and every statement made by the application itself, is true. So long as you have done your best to provide accurate information, feel free to sign. If you're not sure whether some of the statements are true or not, do a little more homework. It's always better to leave something out than to put in information that you know to be false, or which you aren't sure about.

Well, that's it. That's how you fill out an application to have your conviction dismissed. Not so bad, is it? And that's the most difficult part of the whole process.

Now, make sure the form you have torn out is the one you use under Penal Code §1203.4 (the one we described a little earlier) and fill it in as we've suggested in this section. Take your time.

Photocopy Note: Again, we urge you to make a couple of copies of the form before you start filling it out, so that in case you make a mistake, you'll have spares. When you prepare other forms later in this chapter, keep this advice in mind.

Step 2: Prepare Notice of Hearing

Welcome back to those returning from Chapters 8, 9, or 11.

Before you go down to the courthouse to file your papers, you'll need to prepare a couple of additional forms. They're easy so long as you follow our step-by-step instructions. First, you should check with the court clerk to find out if a court hearing is required in your county. If it isn't, you may only need to fill in and file your application and have copies sent to the prosecuting attorney and probation department. If a hearing is required, the first of these forms is called a Notice of Hearing and will let the necessary agencies know of your intentions to get your conviction dismissed.

FILL IN BOXES 1-4

The top part of the Notice of Hearing (Boxes 1-4) should look familiar. It's identical to the application discussed just above, and should be filled out the same way.

FILL IN BOX 5

1. To   ☐ _____ District Attorney for _____ County;
       ☐ _____ City Attorney for _____ City;
       ☐ _____ Probation Department for _____ County;

In this box, you'll be listing the criminal justice agencies who are entitled to receive a copy of your application and notice of the hearing. The first agency to notify is the one that prosecuted you. In felony cases, this will be the district attorney of the county involved in your case. If your conviction was for a misdemeanor, the agency may be the city attorney's office instead of the district attorney. If you're unsure, check with your probation officer and/or your attorney. If that doesn't work, call the court clerk and ask how you can find out.

If the district attorney prosecuted you, check the first box. If the city attorney prosecuted you, check the second box. Only one of these two choices should be selected.

The other agency that needs to be informed is the probation department. Check the third box.

FILL IN BOX 6

> Notice is given that defendant _____ will move the court
> for an order:

Here, you put your name exactly as it
appears on the application and Box 3 of this
form.

FILL IN BOX 7

> ☐ permitting defendant to withdraw or set aside his/her conviction, to
>   dismiss the case, and for relief from all penalties and disabilities
>   pursuant to Penal Code §1203.4;
> ☐ permitting defendant to withdraw or set aside his/her conviction, to
>   dismiss the case, and for relief from all penalties and disabilities
>   pursuant to Penal Code 1203.4a;
> ☐ permitting minor defendant to seal records of misdemeanor conviction in
>   criminal court and other records of offense, pursuant to Penal Code
>   §1203.45;
> ☐ to reduce the offense from a felony to a misdemeanor, pursuant to Penal
>   Code §17.

This box tells the agencies which remedy
you're seeking. Check the first box. In some
situations, you may be seeking more than one
remedy in the same hearing. If you are, you'll
have been sent here from one of the other
chapters (8, 9 or 11), and you should go back to
that chapter to find out which box to check for
the other remedy that applies to you. Unless you
have followed the procedures in any of the other
chapters (8, 9, 11), however, you should leave
the rest of the boxes blank.

FILL IN BOX 8

> 2. A hearing on this matter will be held as follows:

> a. date: time: in ☐ Dept: ☐ Div: ☐ Room:

> b. Address of court:

This box tells the agencies when and where
your hearing will take place. Since you're filling
out this form before you file your application,
you have no idea what to put in. Don't worry.
When you file your papers, the court clerk will
provide you with this information. The address
for the court should be the same as you put in
Box 2, unless the court has a different physical
location from its mailing address. If you aren't
sure about this, call the court clerk and find out.

Now, turn to the Appendix and locate the
Notice of Hearing form. Tear it out. First turn it
over. On the other side, you'll see another form
called "Proof of Service." We discuss that in Step
3, just below. For the moment, you should only
be concerned with the Notice of Hearing side. It
will be wise to photocopy both sides of this form
before beginning work on the one we provide,
just in case you mess up. Fill out the form,

following the instructions we've just been through. Then read the next section.

Step 3: Fill Out Proof of Service

Welcome to those coming from Chapter 13.

The point of a "Proof of Service" form is for the court to be sure you have notified the proper agencies about your application and the date of the hearing. Whenever a court requires persons or agencies to be notified of the hearing, they also require the person requesting the hearing to file a statement under oath that the appropriate papers have been sent or delivered to these agencies. This is called "serving" the papers.

Who can serve the papers? Just about any adult other than you. It can be a friend, relative or anybody else over 18 years of age. Therefore, it will be necessary to get the cooperation of at least one other person. Fortunately, their job is a simple one.

How can papers be served? There are two ways. One is to personally deliver them to the agencies listed in your Notice of Hearing. The other is to mail them to the agencies. Mailing them is obviously easier and most often used for this type of proceeding.

Now, take a look at the Proof of Service form (on the back of the Notice of Hearing). This is the statement you make under oath that the papers have been served. Whoever actually serves the papers must sign this form, and their name must appear as the person doing the serving. However, you can and should fill it out *except* for the dates, the signature of the "server," and location of where the papers were mailed from, if you use the mail method.

As you can see, the form provides for both methods of service (mail and hand delivery). Of course, before you can serve the papers, you'll need to find the location of the agencies in question. Again, the telephone is a good way to do this. The office of the prosecuting attorney and the probation department will probably be at or near the building where the court clerk is located. You could personally serve these papers on the day you file your application if you bring your friendly server along.

Once you have located the addresses of the agencies checked on your Notice of Hearing, put the names and addresses of the agencies in the part of the Proof of Service form labelled Box 11, below;

FILL IN BOX 11

NAME AND ADDRESS OF EACH PERSON TO WHOM NOTICE WAS MAILED OR DELIVERED:

If you're planning to have the papers served personally, put in all the information called for in the part of the form labelled Box 9, below, except the date. Leave the date blank for now.

FILL IN BOX 9

PROOF OF SERVICE

☐   PROOF OF <u>PERSONAL</u> SERVICE

I am over the age of 18 and not a party to this case. I am a resident of or employee in the county of _____. My residence or business address is:

I served the foregoing Notice of Hearing by personally delivering a true copy of the Notice of Hearing and defendant's declaration to each person whose name and address is given below on the date of _____.

I declare under penalty of perjury under the laws of the State of California that the foregoing is true and correct.

_____
(Print name)

_____
(Sign name)

If you're planning to have the papers served by mail, fill in the information called for in the part of the form labelled Box 10, below, except the dates and places.

FILL IN BOX 10

☐   PROOF OF SERVICE <u>BY MAIL</u>

I am over the age of 18 and not a party to this case. I am a resident of or employee in the county where the mailing occurred. My residence or business address is:

I served the foregoing Notice of Hearing and Declaration by enclosing a true copy in a sealed envelope addressed to each person whose name and address is given below and depositing the envelope in the United States mail with the postage fully prepaid.

(1) Date of deposit: (2) Place of deposit (city & state):

I declare under penalty of perjury under the laws of the State of California that the foregoing is true and correct.

(date):_____ at (place): _____, California

_____
(Type or Print Name)

_____
(Signature of Declarant)

At the time you're filling out these forms, you haven't yet filed your papers and don't know when your hearing date will be (we cover this in Step 5, below).

Since the dates on the Proof of Service form tell when you had the papers served (i.e., dropped them in the mail box or actually delivered them to the agencies), you'll have to wait until you file and serve your papers before you can put the dates in the Proof of Service.

If you decide to have one of the agencies served by mail and another by person, separate Box 11 into two sections. Label one "Service by Mail" and the other "Personal Service," and then put the name and address of the agency that was served by each method.

At this time, you should have filled out:

- your application for getting your conviction dismissed (except for the hearing date and location);
- your Notice of Hearing form (except for the hearing date);
- your Proof of Service form (except for the dates, signature and location of mailing).

Now that you've done all this, you deserve to sit back and relax, right? Not yet. Unless you take your application to the court, and file it, nothing will happen. Also, once you take your application and obtain a hearing date, you'll need to serve your application, Notice of Hearing, and file your Proof of Service with the court.

Step 4: Make Copies of Application

This is an easy one. Make photocopies of your application. If you're using more than one remedy, make three copies of each petition or application.

Step 5: File Papers

Now it's time for the trip to the courthouse. While it's possible to do this by mail, as we mentioned earlier, we think it's better to do it in person. If you get something wrong, the clerk will quite often, but not always, help you get it right. Before you go to, or mail anything to, the Court Clerk's office, you should call to find out if there's any filing fee, so you'll know if you need to bring or send a check. If the filing is done by mail, on the other hand, your case may get lost in the incredible paper blizzard that's part of most clerks' offices. If you do mail, make sure you keep an extra copy of all papers, and include a

note asking the clerk to file the original application, pick a hearing date, and return the confirmed copies in the enclosed stamped, self-addressed envelope (don't forget the envelope). Here's a sample of what the letter might say:

May 7, 19__

Dear Clerk:

I want to apply to have my conviction set aside and my case dismissed under Penal Code §1203.4 and would appreciate your filing my application contained in this envelope. In addition to the original, I've enclosed three copies. Please return the file stamped copies in the self-addressed stamped envelope that I've enclosed for your convenience. Also, please send notification of the hearing date and location when and if it's assigned.

A check for the filing fee of $_____ is also enclosed.
                If there are problems with my papers, I would appreciate any guidance you can provide. Thank you for your help.

Sincerely,

No matter how good a job you did on your papers, actually taking them to the courthouse can be a bit scary. After all, this will be the first time somebody will be looking at them to see whether you goofed. Please believe us when we say, "Don't worry." Now, let's get down to business.

Go to the court clerk's office and tell them you want to file your "Application to Get Your Conviction Dismissed." If you're using one of the remedies in another chapter, give that title). There may be one clerk who handles all filing, or there may be a separate clerk for criminal matters to whom you'll be directed. When you find the right clerk, tell him or her what you want and hand in your original application and three copies. At this time, you'll be informed about your hearing date, time and place, or you may be told that you'll be informed at a later time when and where the hearing is to be scheduled.

The clerk will stamp your application, "Filed," in the upper right hand corner, which we left blank because it was labelled "for court use only," and keep the original application. At this time, you should have three copies left. These should also be stamped, "Filed."

Now what? If you have been given a hearing date, time and place, you'll want to enter this information in 1) your copy of the application, 2) the copies of any applications that you need to serve on agencies, and 3) the Notices of Hearings that you're planning to have served. If the clerk can't give you a date, ask what you should do next. You'll probably be told that you'll be informed later. If so, you'll have to go home and wait. But don't wait too long. Check with the court from time to time.

Step 6: Copy Notice of Hearing/Proof of Service

Once you have the information about your hearing, you'll be able to fill in your Notice of Hearing, the time, place and date of the hearing in your petition, and the date on which you'll be serving your papers on the agencies. Go through the following check list to make sure your forms have all the necessary information.

Box 4 of all three copies of your application should have the date, time and place of the hearing filled in:

Boxes 4 and 8 of the Notice of Hearing should also have the date, time, and place of the hearing:

The Proof of Service form should have the name of the person doing the serving, the date the papers will definitely be served, the location where they'll be mailed to (if service is by mail), or delivered to (if personal service is the method you use), and the signature of the person serving them. Once this information is filled in, make three photocopies of the front and back of the Notice of Hearing/Proof of Service form.

Step 7: Serve Papers

Start by making at least three packets. Each packet will consist of copies of your application, the Notice of Hearing, and the Proof of Service (the back of the Notice of Hearing form). One packet must be served on each of the agencies checked off on your Notice of Hearing form.

If service is being done by mail, address envelopes to each of the agencies, place a packet inside the envelope, put first class postage on the envelope, and have your "server" mail it in time to get it postmarked on the date entered in your Proof of Service. For example, if your Proof of Service says you served the papers by mail on January 3, 1984, make sure the letter is mailed in time to get a postmark on this day.

If your papers are being served personally, have your server deliver them to the agencies on the same day indicated on the Proof of Service. They can be left with any responsible person at the agency, who will usually be the receptionist. The server should indicate, however, that they're court papers. The last complete set is for you to keep for your records.

Make sure that all the persons or agencies are served at least 15 days before the date of the hearing.

Step 8: File Proof of Service

At this point, you should still have the original Notice of Hearing/Proof of Service completely filled in. Take it or mail it (in this case, it could be mailed) to the court and get it filed at least five days before the hearing is scheduled.

By filing this document, you'll be telling the court that the necessary agencies have been properly notified and that it's okay to put the matter on the court calendar for hearing.

Are you still with us? Good. There's only one more form to go.

Step 9: Prepare Order Dismissing Conviction

For those of you using other chapters (8, 9, 11 or 13), return to your chapter for good. From here on in, only Chapter 7 people should stay with us.

Sometime before the hearing, you'll need to prepare the Order that the judge will sign, hopefully giving you what you ask for. If no hearing is required in your county, you should deliver this Order to the court clerk's office when you file your application. Attach a self-addressed, stamped envelope so the court will be able to send you a copy of the signed Order.

Find the form labelled "Order Permitting Defendant to Withdraw Conviction to Dismiss The Case, and To Release Defendant From All Penalties and Disabilities Resulting From Offense (Penal Code §1203.4)" in the Appendix and fill it in as we suggest below. (Remember our photocopying suggestion.) After you've filled it in, hold on to it until the day of the hearing. Then make sure you take it, and three copies, with you. When the judge grants your relief, he or she will ask for the Order. If you don't have it prepared, it may mean a delay. If you don't plan to attend the hearing, make sure the original and 3 copies of the Order and a stamped, self-addressed envelope are in the court on or before the hearing date.

FILL IN BOXES 1-4

Follow the instructions in Step 1, Boxes 1-4 of this chapter.

FILL IN BOX 5

```
1. The application for relief under Penal Code §1203.4 filed on
   _____ came on for hearing as follows:
   a. Date:              Dept:         Div:         Room:
   b. Judge (name):                                 ☐ Temporary
   c. ☐ Defendant present in court
   d. ☐ Defendant's attorney present in court (name):
   e. ☐ District Attorney/City Attorney present in court (name):
   f. ☐ Probation officer present in court (name):
   g. ☐
   Copies of the notice of hearing and defendant's application were served on
   all of the above-named offices.
```

In this box, put the date you filed your application, and leave the rest of it blank. The court clerk will fill in those details.

FILL IN BOX 6

2. ☐ Evidence presented to the court.

Leave this box blank. If anybody testifies in the hearing, the court clerk will check it.

FILL IN BOX 7

```
4.  IT IS ORDERED
    a. ☐ Defendant's plea of guilty/nolo contendere is withdrawn and a plea of
          not guilty is entered.
       ☐ The jury's verdict or the court's finding of guilty after the trial of
          the above-entitled action is set aside and vacated.
    b. The case against defendant is hereby dismissed, pursuant to Penal Code
       §1203.4
    c. The defendant is released from all penalties and disabilities resulting
       from the offense(s) of which he/she was convicted, except as otherwise
       expressly provided by law.
       (Applicant is informed that this order does not relieve him/her of the
       obligation to disclose this conviction(s) in response to any direct
       question contained in any questionnaire or application for public office,
       for license by any state or local agency, or for contracting with the
       California State Lottery.)
```

If your conviction was the result of a plea (guilty or nolo contendere), check the first box. If your conviction was a result of a trial, check the second box. Remember: Only one of these two boxes should be checked, and this information should be the same as the box you checked in Box 8 (Step 1) on your application.

The final paragraphs order that your case be dismissed and that you be released from all penalties and disabilities resulting from the offense(s) of which you were convicted. The Order ends with the disclosure required by law that warns that the dismissal doesn't relieve you of your obligation to disclose your "dismissed" conviction when answering any questionnaire or application for a public officem license by any state or local agency, or for contracting with the California State Lottery.

Step 10: Attend Court Hearing

At the time and place of the hearing on your application, the judge will decide whether to grant or deny your request to get your conviction dismissed. The judge:

1) will review your application (all the information about your case and your statements

under penalty of perjury that you qualify to get your case dismissed),

2) review the probation department's report, and

3) check to make sure the prosecuting attorney's office and the probation department have been notified about your application and the hearing (from the Proof of Service). If everything is in order, your request will be granted and the judge will sign the Order.

If you're required to attend the hearing, the judge may ask you or the probation officer who prepared the criminal record investigation for the hearing, a few brief questions to make sure you really qualify. As long as you do, the questioning will be short and the Order will be signed. Congratulations.

Follow-Up Note: Even though the Order is supposed to take care of everything, humans sometimes make mistakes. This is especially true where computers are involved. With the best will in the world, it's sometimes difficult to get information off a computer once it's been put on. Likewise, it's sometimes difficult to put it on when you need it most. For this reason, we strongly suggest you do a little follow-up about six months after the judge signed the Order. In Chapter 2, we tell you how to find out whether you have a record and to get a copy of it. Follow that procedure to see whether your record has really been changed. If not, take the steps suggested in that chapter to get the mistake corrected.

chapter 8

misdemeanor convictions with no probation

A. Introduction

THIS CHAPTER IS FOR ANYONE who was convicted of a misdemeanor and who didn't receive probation as part of his sentence. If you were convicted of a felony, or were placed on probation, go back to Chapter 7, or to Chapter 9 if your felony was a "wobbler." If you're unsure about either probation or the status of your offense, turn back to Chapter 3 (Part C, Questions 3 and 4), for a discussion of these concepts.

If you qualify so far, we'll be asking you a few more questions to make sure you're eligible for this remedy. Then we'll tell you how to obtain it.

Before you get too far into the details of this chapter, let's ask a basic question. What good does it do you to dismiss a misdemeanor conviction? Under the law, when your conviction is "dismissed," you're "released from all penalties and disabilities resulting from the offense, except as otherwise provided by law." This sounds great, but as you'll see, this remedy isn't as complete as it might seem. This law is very similar to the one described in Chapter 7, so go back to Section C of that chapter for a discussion on the practical effects of getting your conviction dismissed. This remedy does provide one important additional benefit. Unlike the remedy in Chapter 7, there's

no requirement that you disclose your dismissed conviction if you're asked about conviction when you apply for a public (government) job or license. It's our opinion that such remedies are well worth pursuing, in spite of their limitations.

In the rest of this chapter, we'll take you through the process step-by-step.

B. Are You Eligible to Have Your Misdemeanor Conviction Dismissed?

NOT EVERYONE WITH A MISDEMEANOR conviction without probation being imposed is eligible for this remedy. Like most other laws, there are some exceptions and limitations. We'll go over the eligibility requirements by pretending we're on a road trip reading signs. If you follow the signs, which are actually specific questions designed to help you assess your situation, and are with us at the end of the trip, you'll be eligible for this remedy. In some situations, you'll have to exit or detour to another chapter, or delay your remedy for awhile until a little more time passes. At the very end of the chapter, we'll provide you with a map summarizing our trip.

1. Were you an adult when you committed your crime?

If you were 18 or older when you did your deed (21 or older, if it was done prior to March 3, 1973), then you're eligible. Otherwise, detour to Chapters 4 or 11 for possible remedies. If you were referred here from Chapter 11, ignore this requirement.

2. Was your case heard in a California adult criminal court?

If so, go on to the next question. However, if your case was heard in any juvenile court, detour to Chapter 4 for the juvenile offense. If your conviction occurred outside of California or in federal court, then you should exit.

3. Were you convicted for failing to obey a traffic officer?

For some reason, the crimes of failing to obey a traffic officer (Vehicle Code §§2800, 2800.1, 2801, or 2803) aren't covered by this remedy. If your record isn't for these crimes, then continue to the next question. If it is, this remedy won't work for you.

4. Were you convicted of possessing marijuana or related crimes?

If so, detour to Chapter 6 for a much better remedy. If you were convicted in 1976 or later for transporting or giving away less than one ounce of marijuana, also turn to Chapter 6 for further guidance.

5. Did you fully comply with the sentence of the court?

In many cases, judges will impose certain requirements on a person convicted of a misdemeanor that are designed to teach him or her a lesson. This may be a fine, restitution,

community work, or even participation in a rehabilitation program of some sort. While the court will normally impose probation in connection with these conditions, it sometimes doesn't. Since you shouldn't be using this remedy if probation was imposed in your case, we'll assume that certain conditions were imposed on you to be supervised directly by the court. So long as you've fully satisfied the requirements of your sentence, you're still eligible for this remedy.

6. Has at least one year passed since your sentence was imposed?

If so, you're still on the freeway. If not, get off now and wait until the year period is up. If you're not sure when your sentence was imposed, the following questions might jog your memory. Did the judge sentence you the same day you entered a guilty or no contest plea? If so, what day was that? Did the judge set a separate day for your sentencing? If so, see if you can recall the date. If your memory remains stubborn, see if you can find the information on your copies of the court papers. Or, check with your former lawyer or the court clerk.

7. Have you been in any trouble since you were sentenced on the conviction you now want to dismiss?

Are you now serving a sentence for any other offense? Have you broken any laws since you were sentenced? Do you have any cases pending against you?

If you answered "no" to these questions, you're still with us and almost through with the journey. If you had to answer yes, there may be problems. Pay close attention.

Were you convicted of another crime that was committed within the one year period following the sentence for conviction you want dismissed? If so, you're not eligible for this remedy.

Are you currently serving a sentence for a conviction that occurred after the one year period expired? If so, you're still eligible for this remedy,[1] but you'll have to wait until you've satisfied all conditions of your current sentence and are discharged from probation (for your current sentence), if any was imposed.

Are you currently facing charges in court? If so, you'll have to wait until they're resolved one way or the other before you can use this remedy. As we've mentioned, if your current charges end in a conviction, you'll have to wait until all requirements are met on that conviction before you can dismiss the earlier conviction. If your current charges end in a dismissal, then you can rejoin us at this point.

Are you still with us? Great, but just to make sure, check the following roadmap.

C. Getting Your Misdemeanor Conviction Dismissed

FOR ALL PRACTICAL PURPOSES, there's little difference between the Chapter 7 remedy and this one. For certain information, we'll be referring you back to Chapter 7, and then bringing you back here for additional steps. It may seem a little confusing, but if you carefully follow our instructions, there should be no problem.

If you want a brief overview of the dismissal process before you begin, see the one at the beginning of Chapter 7, Section D. If you need a review of who might help you out with the

procedures, go back and reread Chapter 3, Part B(1).

D. Which Court Forms to Use

SOME COUNTIES HAVE PRINTED FORM petitions that only require you to fill in the blanks, sign at the bottom, and send them in. If such form petitions exist in your county (the county where your conviction occurred), you'll be able to find them at either 1) the criminal court clerk's office or 2) the probation department section that handles adult criminal court matters. In a few courts, such as the municipal court in Los Angeles, the printed forms used for dismissing your convictions under the procedure described in Chapter 7 are the same as the forms for this procedure. You just check a different box.

Some courts require you to use their forms, if they exist. Even if you don't have to, it's a good idea. If there's no such form, however, we've provided one for you that is representative of the ones in general use. Since our instructions apply to our own form, they may not be exactly what you need for the county form, but they should prove helpful. So, whether you plan on using our form or the county's form, keep reading.

---

[1] *People v. Chandlee* (1979) 90 Cal. App. [3d] Supp. 13.

ELIGIBILITY MAP TO DISMISS MISDEMEANOR CONVICTIONS

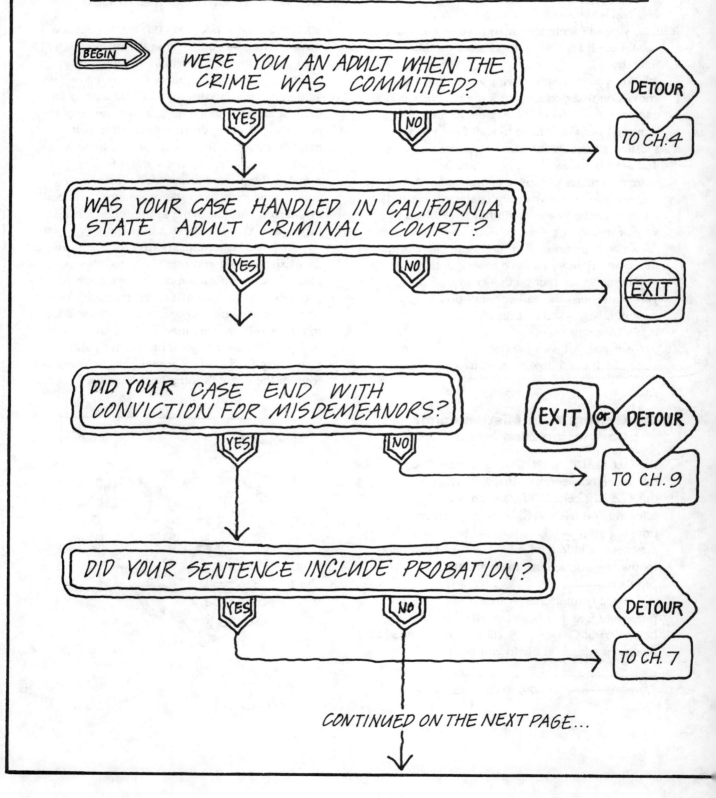

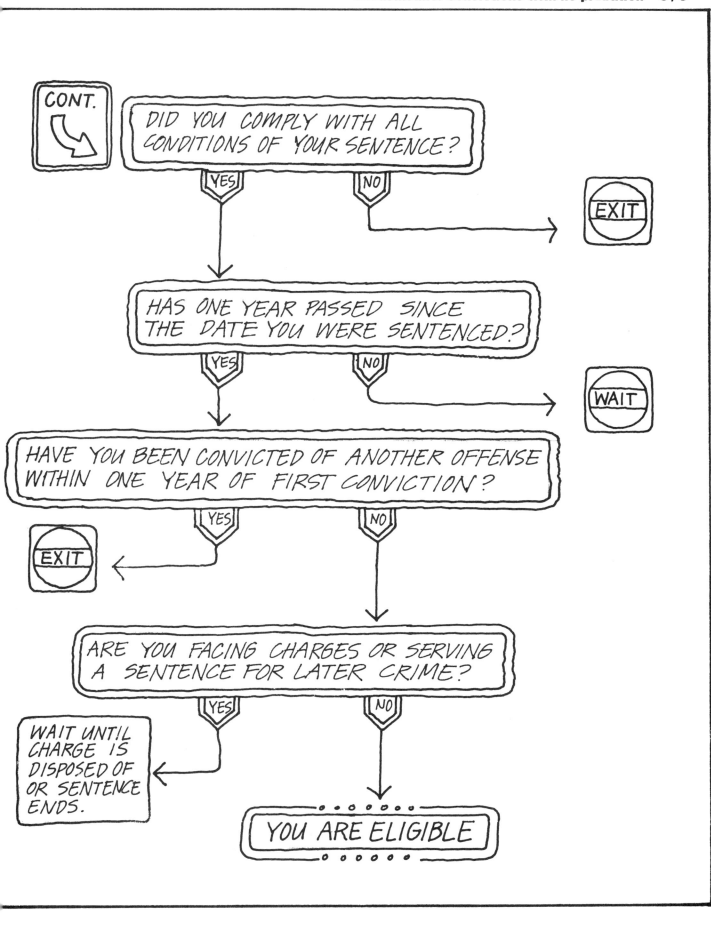

Assuming your county doesn't have its own form, you'll want to use ours. While a lot of the language may seem like Greek, it actually asks for very little information. We'll tell you how to fill it in. Turn to the Appendix and find a blank copy of the form included for your use ("Application to Withdraw Misdemeanor Conviction After One Year Without Probation, To Dismiss the Case, and for Relief From All Penalties and Disabilities Resulting From Offense—Penal Code §1203.4a"). Make sure you have the right form before you tear it out. We recommend you not fill it in until you've carefully read this section. However, if you want to do both at the same time, don't forget to make a photocopy first.

To help you understand our instructions, we've prepared a little story.

Step 1: Fill Out Your Application

Now we'll take the facts from the story and fill in the form, part by part, as an example. Each part is numbered, so when we say "Fill in Box 1," for instance, you'll know what we're referring to. When you finish reading through this example, you'll be entering your own information in the form you removed from the Appendix.

THE SAD STORY OF DON ELLSBURG

Don Ellsburg is strongly opposed to nuclear power plants. He joined hundreds of other anti-nuclear demonstrators for a week of civil disobedience around the Diablo Canyon plant. Don was arrested for trespass (Penal Code §602L). He eventually had a trial on the charge because he hoped to use the trial as a forum to debate nuclear power. The jury convicted Don of trespass. At the sentencing hearing, the judge imposed a sentence of seven days in the county jail and a $250 fine. No probation was imposed. In lieu of the fine, Don was allowed to perform volunteer work at a local hospital. He now wants his conviction dismissed.

FILL IN BOX 1

ATTORNEY OR PARTY WITHOUT ATTORNEY (NAME AND ADDRESS)	TELEPHONE NO
DON ELLSBURG 517 GLOW STREET LIVERMORE, CA 94550	(415) 447-8181
ATTORNEY FOR (NAME) *Defendant DON ELLSBURG, in proper*	

Box 1 is for your name, current address and telephone number. In the case of Don Ellsburg, his address is 517 Glow St., Livermore, California, and his phone number is (415) 447-8181.

Since Don is representing himself, as you'll be doing, we've put him as "Defendant in pro per," which is Latin for "representing yourself."

FILL IN BOX 2

```
MUNICIPAL          COURT OF CALIFORNIA, COUNTY OF  SAN LUIS OBISPO
                          SAN LUIS OBISPO  JUDICIAL DISTRICT
STREET ADDRESS
MAILING ADDRESS    P.O. BOX 1247
CITY AND ZIP CODE  SAN LUIS OBISPO , CA  93406
BRANCH NAME
```

Box 2 contains the information about the court that you're asking to dismiss your conviction. In our story, Don's conviction occurred in the San Luis Obispo County Municipal Court, San Luis Obispo Judicial District. In most large counties, there are several municipal court judicial districts. If you don't know which one was involved in your case, call the court clerk and ask. Usually the names of the cities covered are part of the title. Also, it might be found on any old court papers you may have kept. Finally, you can call your attorney.

Put the word "Municipal" before the word "court," the name of the county where your conviction occurred after "County of," and the name of the judicial district before the words, "Judicial District," on the second line.

This box also requires the address of the court. You can often find this in the phone book, or it may be on your old papers. The court clerk will also tell you over the phone. Make sure you get the correct address. If the mailing address is different than the street address (such as a P.O. Box), fill both addresses in.

If your conviction occurred many years ago, it's a good idea to call to make sure the court hasn't moved or been consolidated.

If your misdemeanor conviction occurred in superior court, fill in the word "superior" before the word "court," and the name of the county where your conviction occurred after the words, "county of." Don't fill in anything on the second line before the words "judicial district." If this superior court has more than one branch, fill in the branch name below the address.

FILL IN BOX 3

```
THE PEOPLE OF THE STATE OF CALIFORNIA
                   vs.
     DON ELLSBURG
                            Defendant
```

This box contains the title of your case. Put your name after the "vs." If you go by more than one name, make sure you put the name your conviction occurred under. Otherwise, the court may get confused and problems may develop.

FILL IN BOX 4

CASE NUMBER	81- 6253
HEARING DATE	
DEPT	TIME

This box contains several items. The case number should be the same as it was on the case that resulted in your conviction. If you no longer remember, or don't have court papers that contain it, call your attorney or the court clerk to get it.

The rest of the box should be left blank at this time. Later on, when you get a hearing date, these items will be filled in.

FILL IN BOX 5

2. On _October 16, 1981_, I was convicted of the following misdemeanor
offense(s): _Trespass (Penal Code Sec. 602L)_

In this box, you need to put the date of your conviction and the actual offense for which you were convicted. In Don's case, he learned from his sentencing papers that his conviction occurred on October 16, 1981, and that he was convicted for the crime of trespass (Penal Code §602L). If he didn't have any papers, he could have obtained this information from his lawyer, or the court clerk.

Remember: The crime(s) you were convicted of may be different from the ones you were originally charged with. Your guilty plea may have been the result of a "plea bargain," where the original charges may have been reduced to a less serious offense. If your case went to trial, a jury or judge may have found you guilty of crimes different from those you were originally charged with.

Items 3-7 of the petition don't call for a response. However, when you later sign the petition, you'll in effect be agreeing that each of these statements is true. If you stayed with us on our road trip in Section B, then you'll be able to agree with these statements.

Don, for example, fully complied with the sentence of the court. He served his jail term and worked off his fine. Don knows the date he was sentenced. It wasn't the same day as his trial. The judge wanted to review his record, so he had to return to court for his sentencing six weeks after the trial. Don counts the one year period from the date of sentencing. If any of the other statements hadn't been true, Don couldn't have used this remedy.

3. I was not put on probation and I have fully complied with and performed the sentence of the court.

4. More than one year has passed since the date of pronouncement of judgment.

5. I am not now serving a sentence for any other criminal offense.

6. I am not now charged with the commission of any offense in any pending criminal case.

7. Since the date of pronouncement of judgment, I have lived an honest and upright life and have conformed to and obeyed the laws of the land.

FILL IN BOX 6

WHEREFORE, applicant moves that:

1. ☐ The court allow me to withdraw my plea of guilty/nolo contendere and to enter a plea of not guilty;
    ☒ The court set aside and vacate the jury's verdict or the court's finding of guilty after the trial of the above-entitled action;

2. The court dismiss this action pursuant to Penal Code §1203.4a.

3. The court order that I be released from all penalties and disabilities resulting from the conviction(s) except as otherwise expressed provided by law.

This box is known as the "prayer," and is very much like the real thing. It informs the court of what you want, and asks that your prayer be granted. In Don's case, he was found guilty by the jury after a trial, so therefore, he checked the second box. However, most convictions result from guilty or no contest pleas, and the chances are pretty good you'll be checking the first box also.

If your conviction resulted from a guilty verdict after trial by judge or jury, as Don's did, you'll want to check the second box. But only check one of these two choices.

FILL IN BOX 7

I declare under penalty of perjury under the laws of the State of California that the foregoing is true and correct.

DATED: *December 7, 1982* ——— *Don Ellsburg* ———
                                           DEFENDANT

In this box, you put the date you're filling out the application, and sign under penalty of perjury. This means that to the best of your knowledge every statement that you made and every statement made by the application itself is true. So long as you've done your best to provide accurate information, feel free to sign. If you're not sure whether some of the statements are true or not, do a little more homework. It's always better to leave something out than to include information that you know to be false or about which you aren't sure.

Well, that's it. That's how you fill out an application to have your conviction dismissed. Not so bad, is it? And that's the most difficult part of the whole process.

Now, double check to make sure you have the right form ("Application to Withdraw Misdemeanor Conviction After One Year Without Probation, To Dismiss the Case, and For Relief From All Penalties and Disabilities Resulting From Offense (Penal Code §1203.4a"), and fill it in as we've suggested in this section. Take your time.

Photocopy Note: Before you start filling out the form, it would be a very good idea to make a couple of copies, so in case you make a mistake, you'll have spares. When you prepare other forms later in this chapter, keep this advice in mind.

Steps 2-8:   Go to Chapter 7, Section E

It's time to turn to Chapter 7, specifically to Section E, beginning with Step 2 ("Preparing the Notice of Hearing Form"). Read Steps 2-8. The only difference between the Chapter 7 remedy and the one we're discussing now is that you'll be checking the second box in the Notice of Hearing form (Step 2).

FILL IN BOXES 1-4

Fill in the same as with the other documents.

FILL IN BOX 5

1. The application for relief under Penal Code §1203.4 filed on
   _____ came on for hearing as follows:
   a. Date: Dept: Div: Room:
   b. Judge (name):   ☐ Temporary
   c. ☐ Defendant present in court
   d. ☐ Defendant's attorney present in court (name):
   e. ☐ District Attorney/City Attorney present in court (name):
   f. ☐ Probation officer present in court (name):
   g. ☐
   Copies of the notice of hearing and defendant's application were served on all of the above-named offices.

In this box, put the date you filed your application, and leave the rest of it blank. The court clerk will fill in those details.

Step 9:   Prepare Order Dismissing Conviction

Welcome back from Chapter 7. We're now ready to complete the last form. Sometime before the hearing, you'll need to prepare the Order that the judge will sign, hopefully giving you what you ask for. If no hearing is required in your county, you should send or deliver this Order to the court clerk's office a short time after you file your application. Be sure to attach a stamped, self-addressed envelope, so the court will send you a copy of the signed Order.

Now, locate the form called "Order Permitting Defendant to Withdraw Misdemeanor Conviction After One Year Without Probation, To Dismiss the Case, and To Release the Defendant From All Penalties and Disabilities Resulting From Offense (Penal Code §1203.4a)" in the Appendix. Tear it out and take a look. The top part of the form is identical to the application and Notice of Hearing. As for the rest of it, we'll take you through it step-by-step, just like we did with the application and Notice of Hearing.

FILL IN BOX 6

    2.☐ Evidence presented to the court.

Leave this box blank. If anybody testifies in the hearing, the court clerk will check it.

FILL IN BOX 7

    4. IT IS ORDERED
        a. ☐ Defendant's plea of guilty/nolo contendere is withdrawn and a plea of
               not guilty is entered.
            ☐ The jury's verdict or the court's finding of guilty after the trial of
               the above-entitled action is set aside and vacated.
        b. The case against defendant is hereby dismissed, pursuant to Penal Code
            §1203.4
        c. The defendant is released from all penalties and disabilities resulting
            from the offense(s) of which he/she was convicted, except as otherwise
            expressly provided by law.

If your conviction was the result of a plea (guilty or nolo contendere), check the first box. If your conviction was the result of a trial, check the second box. But remember, only one of these two boxes should be checked, and this information should be the same as the box you checked in Box 6 on your application.

The final paragraphs order that your case be dismissed and that you be released from all penalties and disabilities resulting from the offense(s) of which you were convicted.

After you've filled in the Order, hold on to it until the day of the hearing. Then make sure you take it and three copies with you. When the judge grants your "prayer," he'll ask for the Order. If you don't have it prepared, it may mean a delay. If you don't plan to attend the hearing, make sure the original and 3 copies of the order and a stamped, self-addressed envelope are in the court on or before the hearing date.

Step 10: Attend Court Hearing

At the time and place of the hearing on your application, the judge will decide whether to grant or deny your request to get your conviction dismissed. The judge will:

1) review your application (all the information about your case and your statements under penalty of perjury that you qualify to get your case dismissed);

2) review the probation department's report; and

3) check to make sure the prosecuting attorney's office and the probation department have been notified about your application and the hearing (from the Proof of Service).

If everything is in order, your request will be granted and the judge will sign the order.

If you're required to attend the hearing, the judge may ask you, or the probation officer who prepared the criminal record investigation for the hearing, a few brief questions to make sure you really qualify. As long as you do (you stayed with us on our little trip earlier in the chapter), the questioning will be short and the Order will be signed.

Follow-Up Note: Even though the Order is supposed to take care of everything, humans sometimes make mistakes. Especially where computers are involved, it's sometimes difficult to get information off a computer once it's been put on. Likewise, it's difficult to put it on when you need it most. For this reason, we strongly suggest you do a little follow-up about six months after the judge signs the Order. In Chapter 2, we tell you how to find out whether you have a record and how to get a copy of it. Follow that procedure to see whether your record has really been changed. If not, take the steps suggested in that chapter to get the mistake corrected.

chapter 9

softening the effects of your felony conviction

A. Reducing Certain Felony Convictions to Misdemeanors

AS YOU PROBABLY KNOW by now, having a felony record is much worse than a record for misdemeanors. While there's that shadowy area of moral turpitude misdemeanors discussed in Chapter 4, it's always harder on you to be an ex-felon. Ex-felons cannot own or possess conceal-able firearms, are automatically barred from many types of jobs, and are at a great disadvantage in the job market. There are other disabilities that may result, depending on your circumstances, as we discussed in Chapter 1, Section B.

Now that we've discussed the bad news, we may have some good news for you. In California, there are over 140 different crimes that may be considered either felonies or misdemeanors. These are called "wobblers," because they wobble from being misdemeanors to felonies, depending on the circumstances, and whether the district attorney decides to charge you with the felony or the misdemeanor. An example of of a wobbler is:

PENAL CODE §273A: WILLFUL CRUELTY OR UNJUSTIFIABLE PUNISHMENT OF CHILD; ENDANGERING LIFE OR HEALTH

(1) Any person who, under circumstances or conditions likely to produce great bodily harm or death, willfully causes or permits any child to suffer, or inflicts thereon unjustifiable physical pain or mental suffering, or having the care or custody of any child, willfully causes or permits the person or health of such child to be injured . . . is punishable by imprisonment in the county jail not exceeding one year, *or* in the state prison for two, four or six years.

The county jail part of the punishment makes the offense a misdemeanor, while the state prison time makes it a felony. Whether or not a person convicted of this type of offense has been convicted of a felony or misdemeanor depends on several important factors:

- If the district attorney charged you with the felony and the judge sentenced you to state prison, then you were convicted of a felony.
- If the district attorney charged you with a felony and upon your conviction the judge sentenced you to probation without time in the state prison *and* declares the offense to be

a misdemeanor, then you were convicted of a misdemeanor.

- If the judge committed you to the California Youth Authority *and* declared the offense to be a misdemeanor, then you were convicted of a misdemeanor. Even if the judge doesn't declare the crime to be a misdemeanor, it shall be considered a misdemeanor for all purposes after your release from the Youth Authority.

If you were convicted of a felony under a wobbler statute, you're entitled to petition the court imposing the sentence to change it to a misdemeanor.

If you believe you were convicted of a felony, you can check with an attorney to find out whether it was a "wobbler." You can also do this yourself if you know the code section under which you were convicted. If, for example, you were convicted under Penal Code §484, locate the penal code in your nearest law library or public library and read the section. If it allows punishment either in the county jail or in state prison, then it's a wobbler. If you were convicted of Section 484b, for example, you were convicted of a wobbler (be sure to check the law for the year you were convicted, as it may be different from this year's law).

Below is a list of some of the more common "wobbler" crimes found in the California laws as of 1989. Assuming you were convicted of a wobbler felony, what can you do to get it reduced to a misdemeanor?

If the judge sentenced you to state prison, but then withheld imposition of the sentence and placed you on probation instead, you or your probation officer are entitled to request the court at any time to reduce the offense to a misdemeanor.

A little earlier in this section, we told you that if the judge put you on probation *and* declared the offense to be a misdemeanor, it would be considered a misdemeanor. Often, however, at the time of sentencing, the judge will refuse to

declare the offense a misdemeanor, even though probation is ordered and imposition of the sentence to state prison is suspended. In such cases, the judge may be willing to change his or her mind *after* you've successfully completed your probation. If this is, in fact, what happened, you may have an excellent chance of getting the offense changed to a misdemeanor.

Note: In some cases, the judge may state that your felony will be reduced to a misdemeanor when your probation ends. If that's the case, you don't need to file an application.

Once your offense is considered a misdemeanor, you're no longer an "ex-felon." For many of you, this will be a great relief.

How judges react to these requests varies from county to county, and your probation officer (you must have been on probation to be eligible for this remedy) or your lawyer will be in the best position to tell you what qualifications the courts require in your area for changing your felony to a misdemeanor.

If your probation has ended at the time you apply to have your felony reduced, you may also want to file an application to dismiss your conviction (expunge your record). If so, turn to Chapter 7 for a discussion of that remedy.

If you're successful in getting your felony reduced to a misdemeanor, the court will send a report to the California Department of Justice and the police department that made the arrest to let them know you have now only been convicted of a misdemeanor. Each of those agencies will (or should) change their records for your case. Once that happens, if you're ever asked whether you were convicted of a felony, you may answer "no." Many employers will refuse to hire an ex-felon, but will hire persons with only misdemeanor convictions on their record.

Gun Note: Remember, this remedy doesn't restore your right to possess certain firearms.

Penal Code	Crime
245a	Assault With a Deadly Weapon
242	Battery
243a	Battery on a Police Officer
243.4	Battery-Sexual
273.5	Battery-Spouse
243.3	Battery-Transit Personnel
337a	Bookmaking
459	Burglary-Second Degree
273a	Child Abuse
280	Child Concealing
278	Child Stealing
12025b	Concealed Weapon Without License by Convicted Felon
182(4)	Conspiracy to Cheat, Defraud or Obtain Money by False Pretenses
288a	Copulation
537	Defrauding Hotel, Restaurant of Over $400
246	Discharging Firearm in Building
503	Embezzlement
266	Enticing Female Under 18 for Prostitution
148.1	False Bomb Report
236	False Imprisonment
476a	Fictitious Check
470, 484f	Forgery, Credit Card Forgery
487, 484g	Grand Theft, Use of Stolen Credit Card for More Than $400 Within a Six-Month Period
192(3)(1)	Involuntary Manslaughter Vehicle
475	Possession of Forged Bill, or Checks
262	Rape of Spouse
496	Receiving Stolen Property
4550	Rescuing a Prisoner
246	Shooting at a Dwelling
532	Theft—False Pretenses
452	Unlawfully Causing Fire
261.5	Unlawful Sexual Intercourse
594	Vandalism—Damages Exceed $5,000

Health & Safety Code	Crime
11368	Forgery or Alteration of a Prescription
11366	Maintaining Place for Purpose of Selling Narcotics
11363	Planting and Harvesting Peyote
11357a	Possession of Concentrated Cannabis (Hashish)

Vehicle Code	Crime
20001	Hit and Run With Personal Injury
10851	Vehicle Theft

B. How to Reduce Your Wobbler Conviction

IF YOU WERE CONVICTED of a wobbler, and your probation officer and/or lawyer believes that your application to reduce your felony would be successful, an application seeking this relief can be filed with the court where you were sentenced. The easiest and cheapest way to do this is to let the probation department handle the paper work. If they won't do it, however, or you would rather do it yourself, we'll show you how. After we show you how to fill out the application, we'll be referring you to Chapter 7 for additional procedures. You may feel a bit like a yo-yo, but if you follow our instructions carefully, there should be no problem.

C. Which Court Forms to Use

IF YOUR COUNTY DOESN'T HAVE its own form, you'll want to use ours. While a lot of the language may seem like Greek, it actually asks for very little information. We'll tell you how to fill it in. Turn to the Appendix and find a blank copy of the form included for your use ["Application of Defendant for the Court to Declare the Offense for which He/She Was Convicted a Misdemeanor after Probation Ends; Order (Penal Code §17(b)(3)"]. Make sure you have the right form before you tear it out. We recommend you not fill it in until you've carefully read this section. However, if you want to do both at the same time, don't forget to make a photocopy first.

Step 1: Fill Out Petition

FILL IN BOX 1

ATTORNEY OR PARTY WITHOUT ATTORNEY (NAME AND ADDRESS)	TELEPHONE NO
ATTORNEY FOR (NAME)	

Fill in your name, current address and telephone number. If you represent yourself, put your name after "Defendant" and add the words "in pro per," which is Latin for "representing yourself."

FILL IN BOX 2

SUPERIOR	**COURT OF CALIFORNIA, COUNTY OF**
STREET ADDRESS	
MAILING ADDRESS	
CITY AND ZIP CODE	
BRANCH NAME	

Box 2 contains the information about the court that you're asking to reduce your felony conviction. Find out what branch your superior court was, and put it in after the words "Branch Name." Put the name of the county where your conviction occurred after "County of."

This box also requires the address of the court. You can often find this in the phone book, or it may be on your old papers. The court clerk will also tell you over the phone. Make sure you get the correct address. If the mailing address is different than the street address (such as a P.O. Box), fill in both addresses.

FILL IN BOX 3

```
THE PEOPLE OF THE STATE OF CALIFORNIA
                 vs.

                              Defendant
```

This box contains the title of your case. Put your name after the "vs." If you go by more than one name, make sure you put the name your conviction occurred under. Otherwise, the court may get confused and problems may develop.

FILL IN BOX 4

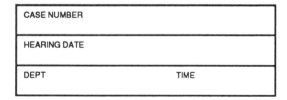

CASE NUMBER	
HEARING DATE	
DEPT	TIME

This box contains several items. The case number should be the same as it was on the case that resulted in your conviction. If you no longer remember, or don't have court papers that contain it, call your probation officer, attorney, or the court clerk to obtain it.

The rest of the box should be left blank at this time. Later on, when you get a hearing date, these items will be filled in.

FILL IN BOX 5

> 2. On _____, I was convicted of the following felony
>   offense(s):
>
>   This crime is punishable by imprisonment, county jail, or fine.

Fill in the date you were convicted and the actual felony offenses for which you were convicted. The last sentence of this paragraph must be true. Remember, wobbler crimes are those punishable by either prison *or* county jail.

FILL IN BOX 6

> 3. As a result of that conviction, I was put on probation and my period
>   of probation ended on _____.

This box requires the date when your probation ended. Check with your lawyer or probation officer if you're not sure of any of the information asked for in the boxes described above. Although the law permits you to apply to reduce your felony wobbler to a misdemeanor any time once you're on probation (you don't have to wait until probation ends), if the judge wasn't willing to declare the offense a misdemeanor at the sentencing, he or she probably will want to see how you did during probation before agreeing to the reduction. Therefore, we feel you should wait until your probation ends if you start this process without a lawyer.

FILL IN BOX 7

> I declare under penalty of perjury under the laws of the State of California
> that the foregoing is true and correct.
>
> DATED: _____
>   DEFENDANT

Put the date you're filling out the petition and sign under penalty of perjury. This means that to the best of your knowledge every statement that you made and every statement made by the petition itself is true. So long as you've done your best to provide accurate information, feel free to sign. If you're not sure whether some of the statements are true or not, do a little more homework. It's always better to leave something out than to include information that you know to be false or about which you aren't sure.

That's all there is to filling out an application to have your felony conviction reduced to a misdemeanor.

Now, make sure the form you've removed from the Appendix is the correct one (look for the words "Petition" and "Penal Code §17(b)(3)," and fill it out as we've suggested in this section. Take your time.

Important Direction: The time has come for you to go to Chapter 7 and follow the instructions there for how to get the court to consider your petition. You've already finished Step 1, but for Steps 2-10, you'll be using Chapter 7. Since there are small differences between the forms and the remedies, however, we've provided a few extra instructions below to help you use Chapter 7. Read them over once, and then turn to the appropriate place in Chapter 7 and follow the steps. If you get a little confused, you can turn back to these instructions.

Step 2

Follow all instructions for Step 2 in Chapter 7, *except* you'll be checking the fourth square in Box 7 of the Notice of Hearing Form.

Steps 3-8

Follow all the instructions in Chapter 7 for Steps 3-8, *except* that your application is to "reduce your felony to a misdemeanor," and not one to "dismiss your conviction."

    Note: Some of you'll be using the remedy in this chapter and in Chapter 7 at the same time. For example, you might want to get your wobbler felony reduced to a misdemeanor, and get the conviction dismissed under Chapter 7. If you're doing both remedies, be sure to photocopy and serve *both* applications and list *both* remedies on your Notice of Hearing. How this is done is covered in Chapter 7.

Step 9

Omit Step 9 in Chapter 7.

Step 10

Step 10 in Chapter 7 should be followed exactly.

D. Other Remedies For Ex-Felons

THERE ARE OTHER AVENUES for convicted felons to soften the effects of their records besides the remedies discussed in Chapter 7 and the one here, which only applies to wobblers [Penal Code §17(b)(3)].

1. Certificate of Rehabilitation

If you were convicted of a felony, you may apply for a Certificate of Rehabilitation by filing a petition in the superior court in the county you're now living in (Penal Code §4852.06). There are certain periods of time to wait between the time you were released from prison, or discharged from probation or parole, before you can apply for the certificate. During that waiting period, you have to lead a law abiding life.

    The law requires all rehabilitative agencies, such as the probation, parole, and youth authority agencies, to assist you in obtaining a Certificate of Rehabilitation, assuming you're eligible, and you're entitled to be represented at the hearing on your petition free of charge (Penal Code §4852.04). To find out how to get this representation in your county, check with your probation officer, attorney, or the public defender's office. The forms for this procedure are available at your county clerk's office at no charge to you.

    If your petition is successful, the court shall declare you rehabilitated and recommend that the governor grant a full pardon (Penal Code §4852.13). While the Certificate of Rehabilitation doesn't remove your felony record for purposes of obtaining a professional or occupational license, the law does provide that a person with a Certificate of Rehabilitation shall not be denied a license *solely* on the ground of the felony record. (Business & Professions Code §480b).

2. Pardons

A certified copy of the Certificate of Rehabilitation sent to the governor constitutes an application for a full pardon. The governor then has the power to pardon you unless you were convicted of two or more felonies. In that case, you need a recommendation from the California Supreme Court before the governor can pardon you (Penal Code §4852.16).

A pardon based on a Certificate of Rehabilitation does restore certain other rights taken away from you because of your felony status. For instance, the pardon restores your right to possess a gun, *unless* your conviction involved the use of a dangerous weapon in the first place. (Penal Code §§4852.17, 4854). And it ends your registration requirement for certain sex and narcotics offenses (Penal Code §290.5).

However, your conviction isn't erased by a Pardon, and the conviction must still be disclosed in job applications and it can be used to increase punishment if you're later convicted of another crime.

3. Reprieves, Pardons, and Commutations

In addition to pardons, the governor has the authority to grant reprieves and commutations of sentence to persons who apply directly to the governor's office (Penal Code §4800). A statement of fact with a recommendation may be requested from the judge or district attorney (Penal Code §4803). A lawyer or other person may receive compensation for assisting in the procuring of a pardon, reprieve, or commutation, but they must file a statement of the amount of the compensation within 10 days of receipt (Penal Code §4807.3).

When the governor grants a full pardon, certain civil rights are restored, but it doesn't remove the conviction for the purpose of obtaining any professional or occupation license (Penal Code §4853), and the possession of certain firearms by people convicted of a felony involving the use of a dangerous weapon is still illegal (Penal Code §4854).

Anyone receiving a pardon who can prove their innocence of the crime for which they were convicted may file a claim for indemnification (payment) for economic injury with the Board of Control for up to $10,000 (Penal Code §§4900, 4901, 4904).

Persons convicted of federal crimes may apply for a presidential pardon through the Pardon Attorney, Department of Justice, Washington D.C. 20530.

chapter 10 ———————————

adult arrest and detention records

A. Introduction

IF YOU WERE EVER ARRESTED or detained, but not convicted, and you're able to prove you were innocent of the crime for which you were suspected, you're eligible to have your arrest or detention record totally wiped out. Unfortunately, though Perry Mason always managed to prove his clients' innocence, it isn't so easy for the rest of us. This remedy, accordingly, seems a bit like Alice's difficulties navigating through Wonderland. Nevertheless, many people will want to use this remedy to wipe out an arrest record.

Warning: There's much uncertainty about this law. Some people think it may be unconstitutional to require people to prove their innocence in order to get their arrest or detention records wiped clean, since everyone is "presumed innocent until proven guilty," in the first place. Further, even if you were totally innocent of the charges for which you were arrested or detained, you might want to think twice about trying to establish your innocence through this remedy. Why? Because, if you make the wrong statements, the police may start to suspect you all over again for that or some other offense. Attorneys commonly tell their clients never to talk to the police, due to the tendency of the police to take everything in its most suspicious light and interpret the most innocent sounding statement as an admission of guilt. Nevertheless, some of you will want to do everything possible to wipe your slate clean. In this chapter, we'll explain who's eligible to use this remedy and what the benefits are. If you do want to follow through, we suggest you hire a lawyer to:

1) advise you on whether you should do it, and

2) get you started or represent you at the hearing. (See Chapter 3, Section B(1) for a few words about lawyers.)

Note: There are two different ways of proceeding under this remedy, depending on whether or not you were charged with a crime. Under California law (Penal Code §849.5), if you were arrested and then released without being charged, your arrest is regarded as merely a detention. If you were never charged, you don't have an arrest record, and may not want to bother getting your detention record sealed. On the other hand, maybe even a detention record bothers you. If so, we'll tell you how it can be wiped out. For the sake of simplicity in this chapter, when we use the word "arrest," we also mean "detention." We'll trust you to distinguish between a detention (no charges filed) and a true arrest (charges filed). As a general matter, detention records don't have the serious consequences arrest records have, since no one ever asks about them.

B. Are You Eligible To Wipe Out Your Arrest Record?

NOT EVERYONE IS ELIGIBLE to use this record sealing law. Like most laws, there are exceptions and limitations. We'll go over the eligibility requirements here.

Requirement #1: You must have been an adult when you were arrested in order to use this remedy. This means you were over 18 (over 21 if your arrest occurred before March 3, 1973). If you weren't an adult, turn to Chapter 4 or 12 for possible remedies.

Requirement #2: You can't have been convicted of any offense connected with your arrest. You were convicted if you entered a guilty plea, a no contest plea, or were found guilty after a trial by a judge or jury. If none of these events happened, you weren't convicted. For more discussion about convictions, turn to Chapter 3, Part C, Questions 3 and 4. If you were convicted, turn to Chapter 7 for a possible remedy. If your conviction was for marijuana possession or certain other minor marijuana crimes, turn to Chapter 6 for an excellent remedy, assuming you qualify.

Hung Jury Note: Sometimes a jury is unable to decide whether a defendant is guilty. If it reports back to the judge that it cannot decide the question of guilt or innocence, the judge will dismiss the jury and declare a mistrial. The jury is said to be "hung" in such a situation. If your case ended because of a hung jury, you're not eligible for this remedy, unless the prosecuting attorney then dismissed all charges against you.

Requirement #3: Can you prove your innocence of the crimes for which you were arrested? In order to use this remedy, you must prove you were actually and "factually innocent" of the crime(s) for which you were arrested (this remedy doesn't apply to infractions such as minor traffic offenses like speeding, etc). In some cases

this may be easy, as in an admitted case of mistaken identity. For example, one person well known around Nolo Press was almost arrested as a prime suspect in a series of local bank robberies. After an hour's detention, the mistake in identity was discovered and no arrest was made. However, sometimes these types of mistakes aren't discovered until after a person has been arrested and charged. In those situations, the factual innocence of the person can be established with relative ease.

In most other cases, however, it's difficult to establish innocence. The fact that you weren't convicted doesn't establish your innocence. Even an acquittal at trial won't do it.[1] Cases are dismissed for all kinds of reasons unrelated to the truth or falsity of the charges brought, and juries may acquit because the prosecutor failed to do his job rather than because they believed you to be innocent. Sometimes, cases are dismissed or acquittals obtained because the victim or accusing witness is unable or unwilling to testify.

> ### EXAMPLE
> A person was recently charged with malicious mischief, but the case was dismissed when the person paid the victim for the damage and the victim decided not to "press charges." The person's request to have his arrest record sealed was denied by the court on the ground that the settlement between the person and the victim didn't indicate factual innocence.[2]

To use this remedy, you have the job of actually proving your innocence. That's one of the main reasons we think you'll probably need a lawyer to be successful with it.

---

[1] *People v. Scott M.* (1985) 167 Cal. App. [3d] 688.
[2] However, if the prosecuting attorney agrees to your request to get your arrest records sealed after your case is dismissed due to a settlement with the victim, your arrest records will be sealed without a finding of factual innocence. *People v. Frank A.M.* (1985) 163 Cal. App. [3d] 939.

Requirement #4: Have less than two years passed since the arrest or the date criminal charges were filed against you? If so, you're still eligible for this remedy. If not, you may be barred from using it. If this requirement causes a problem, you should contact a lawyer to find out whether there are exceptions in your situation.

If no criminal charges were filed against you, you must start this remedy within two years of the detention (no arrest occurred because no charges were brought).

If criminal charges were filed against you, were they filed after your arrest? If so, the two year period starts from the date the charges were filed. If the charges were filed before your arrest, then the date starts with your arrest.

If you're still with us, you're eligible for this remedy. Take a look at the following map for a double check.

C. What Happens to Your Record After It's Sealed?

IF YOUR PETITION IS SUCCESSFUL, the law enforcement agency which arrested you is required to seal your record until three years after your arrest, and then destroy it, along with your petition.

The arresting or detaining agency must also notify the Department of Justice in Sacramento, and any other law enforcement agency that has a record of your arrest, to seal their records for this three year period and then destroy them. If either the Department of Justice or the arresting or detaining agency gave your arrest record to any local, state or federal agency, or to any other person or entity, that person or agency shall be notified and told to destroy your arrest record.

If any record of your arrest is part of any "investigative" police reports, the notation "exonerated" must appear whenever reference is made in these reports to your arrest.

The arresting agency must notify you when your records are sealed and destroyed. You'll also receive a Declaration of Factual Innocence, filled in either by the arresting agency or the court clerk, to show you've been found innocent of the crime.

Once your records have been ordered sealed, the law states "the arrest shall be deemed not to have occurred" and you "may answer accordingly to any question related to its occurrence."

If you're eligible, and you believe the benefits are worth pursuing, contact a lawyer who specializes in criminal law to either represent you or explain the procedure to petition to get your arrest record sealed.

If you cannot afford a lawyer, you might ask the public defender's office if they'll represent you in this procedure. If they represented you after the charges were filed, they may view this remedy as part of their continuing obligation to represent you at all stages of the criminal proceeding. If no charges were filed, or they didn't represent you when charges were filed, it's unlikely they'll handle it for you.

If you want to do it yourself, and need some instructions and forms for completing this procedure, send $10 to Nolo Press, 950 Parker St., Berkeley, California 94710, and say you want to purchase the "Factual Innocence" kit.

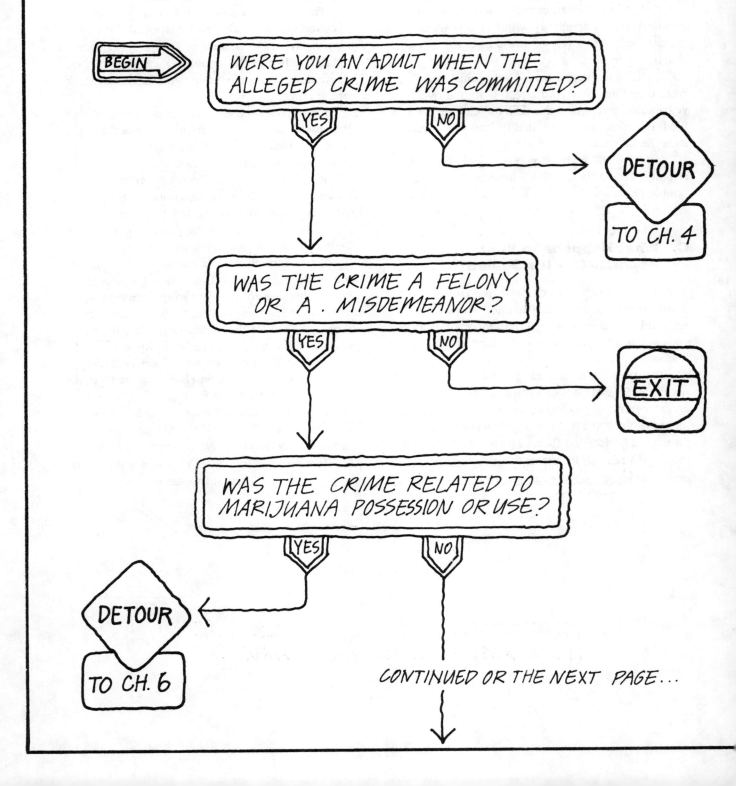

ELIGIBILITY MAP TO
DESTROY ARREST RECORDS

BEGIN →

WERE YOU AN ADULT WHEN THE
ALLEGED CRIME WAS COMMITTED?

YES   NO

→ DETOUR

TO CH. 4

WAS THE CRIME A FELONY
OR A . MISDEMEANOR?

YES   NO

→ EXIT

WAS THE CRIME RELATED TO
MARIJUANA POSSESSION OR USE?

YES   NO

DETOUR ←

TO CH. 6

CONTINUED OR THE NEXT PAGE...

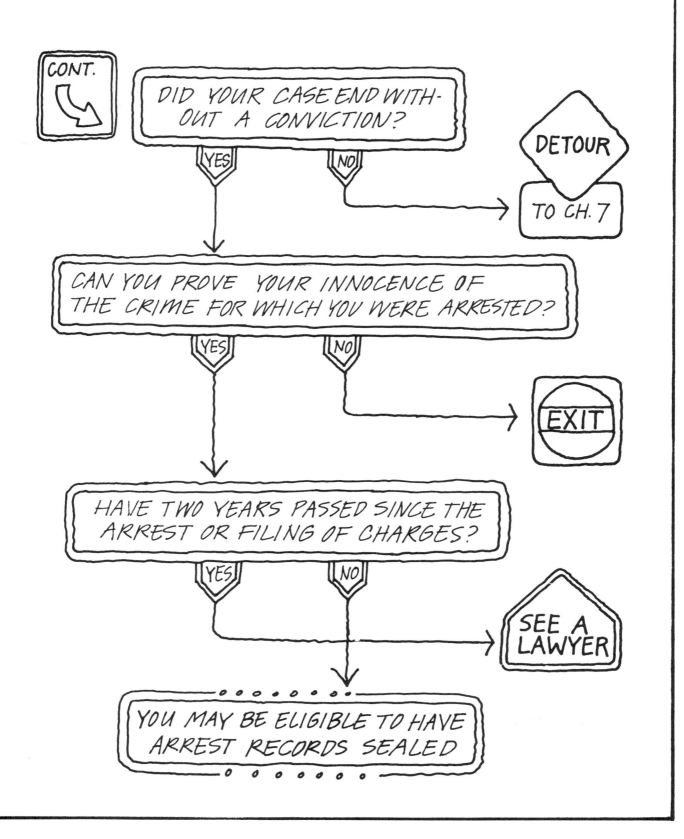

chapter 11 —————————————————

juvenile misdemeanor convictions

IF YOUR CASE WAS TRANSFERRED from juvenile court to adult criminal court because you were found unfit for juvenile court treatment, you may be eligible to have your records sealed. The remedy described in this chapter applies to a very small number of cases, however. Please read the next section carefully, to make sure we can help you here. We don't want you struggling through this process only to get to court and find out you were never eligible to begin with. The vast majority of juvenile court cases involving misdemeanor charges stay in juvenile court, and if your case remained there, go straight to Chapter 4 for your record sealing remedy.

A. Are You Eligible to Get Your Misdemeanor Conviction Record Sealed?

LIKE MOST OTHER LAWS, there are exceptions and limitations on who can use this remedy; the exceptions and limitations will unfortunately disqualify most people. We'll go over the eligibility requirements by pretending we're on a road trip and following road signs to get to the right place. The road signs are actually questions, specifically designed to help you assess your situation. If you're still with us at the end, you're

eligible to get your record sealed. After the written directions, we've included a map, just so you can double check that you followed all the signs.

1. Were you a minor when you committed your crime?

The legal age of adulthood is 18 or older, unless your offense was committed before March 3, 1973, in which case it was 21 or older. If you weren't a minor on the date of the crime for which you were convicted, detour to Chapter 7, which discusses dismissing your adult criminal conviction. If you answered "yes" to our first question, keep going.

2. Did your case end in a California criminal court?

If your case stayed in a juvenile court, detour to Chapter 4. If your case ended in a California adult criminal court because it was transferred from juvenile court after a fitness hearing, then you're still on the trip.

3. Did your case end with your being convicted of only one misdemeanor?

Your case must have ended with you being *convicted* of only one crime. Remember, you were convicted of a crime if you:

- entered a guilty plea
- entered a no contest plea (nolo contendere)
- were found guilty by a judge or jury after trial.

If you weren't convicted of any offense, detour to Chapter 12 or Chapter 4 for a possible remedy. If you were arrested and charged with a felony, but not convicted, one court decision[1] held you may use this remedy to seal your records. Most people in that situation can more easily get their records sealed by using the procedure described in Chapter 4. However, if you were arrested for a felony, but cannot use the Chapter 4 remedy because of another criminal conviction, contact a lawyer about the possibility of using this law to seal your arrest records.

You can only have been convicted of one misdemeanor, to be eligible for this remedy. If you don't know whether your conviction was for a felony or misdemeanor, read Chapter 3(C)(4). If you still don't know, call the attorney who represented you and ask. The main point here is, if you were convicted of more than one misdemeanor, you're not eligible.

4. Did the misdemeanor conviction involve sex, drugs or automobiles?

There are a small number of crimes for which this remedy won't apply. The first are crimes involving failure to obey a traffic officer. Why these? Your guess is as good as ours.

In addition, this remedy doesn't apply to convictions for sex offenses that require you to register under §290 of the Penal Code.

---

[1] *McMahon v. Municipal Court* (1970), 6 Cal. App. [3d] 194.

Drug offenses listed in §11000 of the Health & Safety Code are off bounds also.

Finally, offenses related to state or local laws governing operating, standing, stopping or parking a car are similarly not affected by this remedy.

If any of these exceptions fit your case, check with a lawyer before trying to use this remedy.

If your conviction was for possessing marijuana, detour to Chapter 6. The remedy there is much more effective than the one provided for in this chapter.

5. Have you been in any trouble since this misdemeanor conviction?

In order to get your record sealed by using this law, you need to have almost a spotless record of behavior since that case ended. If any of the following types of trouble apply to you, it's time to exit:

- You have another criminal conviction on your record;
- You're facing charges on another crime.

If you're facing criminal charges on a new case that's still pending, you must wait until the outcome of that case has been determined. If that case ends with the charges being dismissed, you can then come back to this remedy.

6. If you were placed on probation, has your probation ended, and did you successfully complete your probation?

If you weren't placed on probation, go to Question 7.

Probation Note: In Chapter 3, we described probation as having to meet certain conditions in order to avoid spending all of your sentence in jail. If you had a probation officer, then, of course, you were on probation. But it's also possible you were on probation without having to report to anyone (called "summary," "informal" or "court" probation). If you're unsure whether you were on probation, check with the court where you were convicted.

In most cases you cannot apply for this remedy until your probation has ended. Your probation would have ended either when the period of probation imposed on you expired, or, if you were discharged from probation on an earlier date. If you're on probation now, however, and still want to get your record sealed without waiting, contact your probation officer or your attorney. Sometimes the "interests of justice" will permit you to use this remedy even if you're still on probation.

Being eligible to get your records sealed is one of the rewards for performing all the conditions of your probation. For example, if you were required to pay restitution, or participate in a drug rehabilitation program, or to faithfully report to your probation officer, you must have done so in order to use this remedy. If there's evidence that you didn't successfully complete your probation conditions, then this remedy may be denied you. If you were on probation, skip the next question.

7. If you weren't put on probation, has one year passed since the date of your sentencing, and did you comply with all the terms of your sentence?

Being eligible to get your records sealed is one of the rewards for doing well and performing all the requirements of your sentence. You must have fully complied with and performed the sentence of the court. For example, if your sentence required that you pay restitution to a victim, or a fine to the court, or participate in some form of community service or drug/alcohol or vocational counseling, you must have done so and/or paid the amount in full.

There's a one year waiting period before you can apply to the court to seal your misdemeanor conviction. The reason you have to wait is so the court can have a basis for believing you're rehabilitated.

In most misdemeanor cases, your sentencing will have occurred on the same day you were convicted. Sometimes, however, the sentencing is moved to a different day. Find out when you were sentenced and make sure one year has passed, before you start this remedy (assuming you weren't placed on probation).

If you answered "yes" to Questions 1-4, "no" to 5, and "yes" to either 6 or 7, you're eligible to get your misdemeanor conviction records sealed. If you want to double check the route we've just taken, take a look at the following map.

B. What Records Can Be Sealed?

IF YOUR PETITION IS SUCCESSFUL and the court orders your records sealed, all of your records will be sealed. This includes the record of your misdemeanor conviction and other "official" records of the case, including records of your arrest, and "records relating to other offenses" that you may have been charged with, but not convicted of.

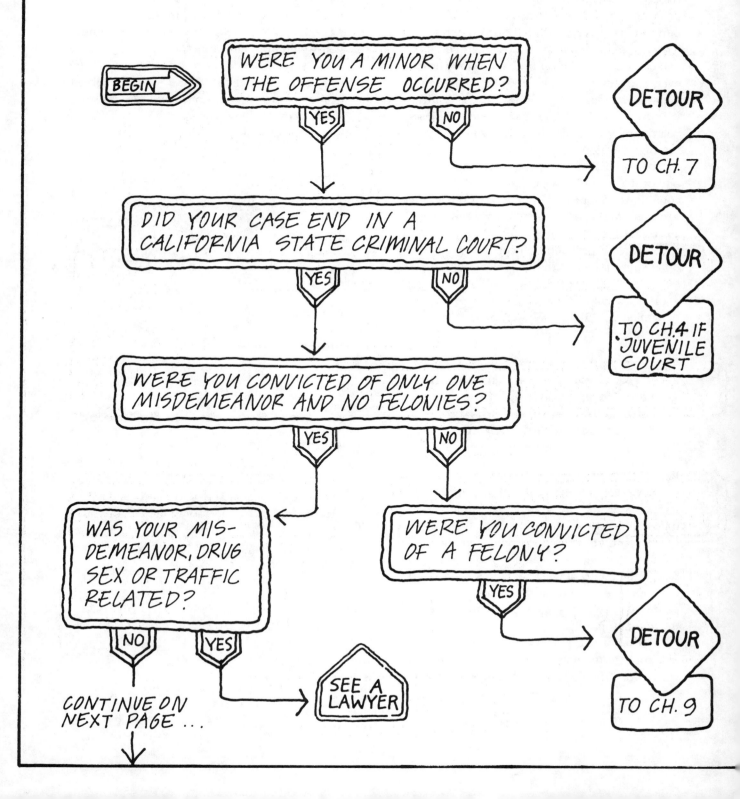

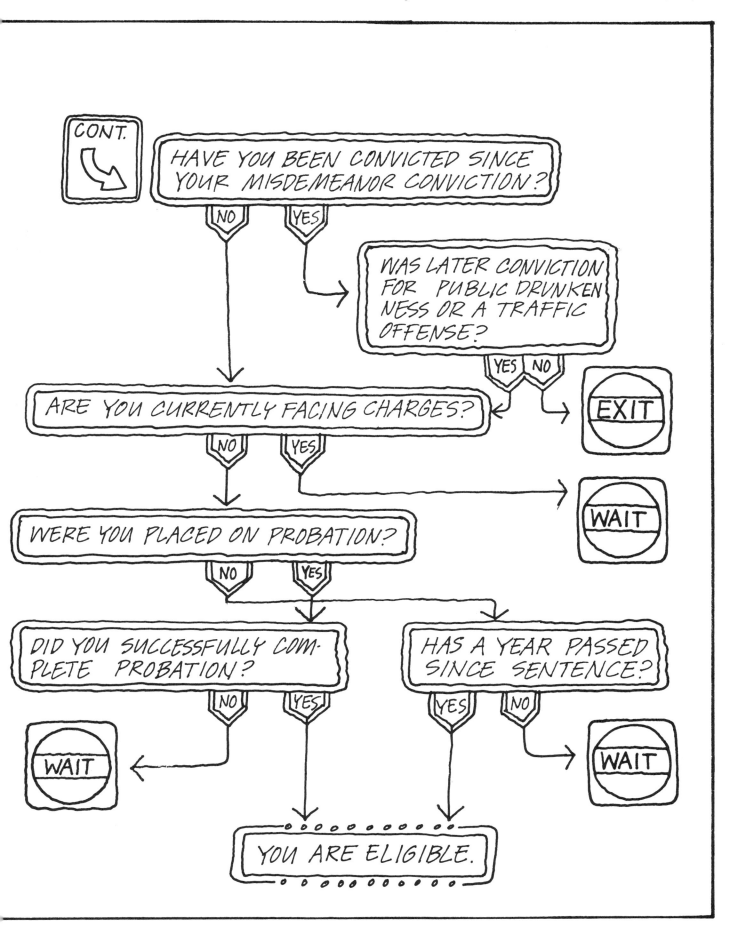

C. Benefits of Record Sealing

ONCE YOUR RECORDS ARE ORDERED sealed by the court, the record sealing law states "thereafter" your "conviction, arrest or other proceeding shall be deemed "not to have occurred" and you may answer "no" if you're ever asked whether you've been convicted of a crime.

A sealed misdemeanor conviction may no longer be used as grounds to deport you (in the event the misdemeanor involved moral turpitude).[2]

Once the Department of Justice receives the court disposition report that your records have been ordered sealed, they'll notify all agencies and offices that had received records of your case and tell them to seal your records. If they're ever asked about your record, they're instructed to answer, "we have no record under that name."

D. How To Start the Procedure

FOR ALL PRACTICAL PURPOSES, there's little difference between the Chapter 7 remedy and this one. Since there are different legal authorities and qualifications for these two remedies, however, we've provided a separate chapter for this one. For certain information, we'll be referring you back to Chapter 7, and then bringing you back here to take the next step or two. It may seem a little confusing, but if you carefully follow our instructions, there should be no problem.

Note: If need be, reread Chapter 3 Part B(1) for information about who might help you with this process. The only parts of that section that are different for this remedy are that:

1) you might want to see a lawyer about the specific eligibility requirements for this remedy, and

2) you should tell the probation department that you want their assistance to get your records sealed under Penal Code §1203.45.

---

[2]*Matter of Lima* (1976) 15 I & N Dec. 661.

E. Which Court Forms To Use

SOME COUNTIES HAVE PETITIONS that only require you to fill in the blanks, sign at the bottom, and send them in. If such form petitions exist in your county (the county where your conviction occurred), you'll be able to find them at either 1) the criminal court clerk, or 2) the probation department section that handles juvenile court matters. Some courts require you to use their forms, if they exist. Even if you don't have to, it's a good idea.

If there's no such form, however, we've provided one for you that is representative of the ones in general use. Since our instructions apply to our own form, they may not be exactly what you need for the county form, but they should prove helpful. So, whether you plan on using our form or the county's, keep reading.

You'll want to use our form if there are no official county ones. While a lot of the language may seem like Greek, it actually asks for very little information. We'll tell you how to fill it in. Turn to the Appendix and find a blank copy of the form, included for your use ("Petition to Seal Minor's Records of Misdemeanor Conviction in Criminal Court and Other Records of Offense— Penal Code §1203.45). Make sure you have the right form before you tear it out. We recommend you not fill it in until you've carefully read this section. However, if you want to do both at the same time, don't forget to make a photocopy first.

To help you understand our instructions, we've prepared a little story.

THE SAD STORY OF TERRY THORN

Terry Thorn and a friend found his father's shotgun. They decided to try some target practice, using a few cans in a nearby park. From there, things went downhill. They were dared by some spectators to shoot at a light fixture in the park clubhouse, and did so, until they realized that people were inside. The police were called, and Terry and his friend were arrested. Since Terry was 17 at the time, a juvenile court petition was filed to declare Terry a ward of the court.

Because the crime involved was a serious one (discharge of a firearm into an occupied building), a "fitness" hearing was held, and Terry's case was transferred to criminal court. There were some problems with the prosecution's case, and Terry eventually plead guilty to one misdemeanor assault charge (Penal Code §241a). Terry was placed on probation for two years, had to attend 10 weekends at a "citizenship training" camp, and couldn't use a gun while on probation. Terry's probation has ended, he has complied with all the probation conditions, and he now wants to seal his misdemeanor conviction record, and the record related to the original charges (which were felonies).

Step 1: Fill Out Petition

Now we'll take the facts from the story and fill in the form, part-by-part as an example. Each part is numbered, so when we say, "Fill in Box 1," for instance, you'll know what we're referring to. After you're through with this example, you'll be putting your own information in the form that you removed from the Appendix.

FILL IN BOX 1

ATTORNEY OR PARTY WITHOUT ATTORNEY (NAME AND ADDRESS)	TELEPHONE NO
TERRY THORN 217 DIABLO BLVD. PITTSBURG, CA 94565	(415) 458-1770
ATTORNEY FOR (NAME) TERRY THORN, in proper	

Box 1 is for your name, current address and telephone number. In the case of Terry Thorn, his address is 217 Diablo Blvd., Pittsburg, California and his phone number is (415) 458-1770.

Since Terry is representing himself, as you'll be doing, we've put him as "Defendant in pro per," which is Latin for "representing yourself."

FILL IN BOX 2

```
┌──────────────────────────────────────────────────────────────────┐
│  MUNICIPAL        COURT OF CALIFORNIA, COUNTY OF  CONTRA COSTA      │
│                              DELTA         JUDICIAL DISTRICT        │
│   STREET ADDRESS                                                   │
│   MAILING ADDRESS   P.O. BOX 431                                   │
│   CITY AND ZIP CODE  PITTSBURG, CA  94565                          │
│   BRANCH NAME                                                      │
│                                                                    │
└──────────────────────────────────────────────────────────────────┘
```

Box 2 contains the information about the court that you're asking to seal your records. In our story, Terry's conviction occurred in the Contra Costa County Municipal Court, Delta Judicial District. Since your conviction was for a misdemeanor, it was probably handled in municipal court. In most large counties, there are several municipal court judicial districts. If you don't know which one was involved in your case, call the court clerk and ask. Also, it might be found on any old court papers you may have kept. Finally, you can call your former probation officer or attorney.

Put the word "municipal" before the word "court," the name of the county where your conviction occurred after "County of," and the name of the judicial district before the words "Judicial District" on the second line.

This box also requires the address of the court. You can often find this in the phone book, or it may be on your old papers. The court clerk will also tell you over the phone. Make sure you get the correct address. If the mailing address is different from the street address (such as a P.O. Box), fill in both addresses.

If your misdemeanor conviction occurred in superior court, fill in the word "superior" before the word "court," and the name of the county where your conviction occurred after the words "county of." Don't fill in anything on the second line before the words "judicial district." If this superior court has more than one branch, fill in the branch name below the address.

FILL IN BOX 3

```
┌──────────────────────────────────────────────────────────────────┐
│   THE PEOPLE OF THE STATE OF CALIFORNIA                            │
│                    vs.                                             │
│        TERRY THORN                                                 │
│                              Defendant                            │
└──────────────────────────────────────────────────────────────────┘
```

This box contains the title of your case. Put your name after the "vs." If you go by more than one name, make sure you put the name your conviction occurred under. Otherwise, the court may get confused and problems may develop.

FILL IN BOX 4

CASE NUMBER	*76521*
HEARING DATE	
DEPT	TIME

This box contains several items. The case number should be the same as it was on the case that resulted in your conviction. If you no longer remember, or don't have court papers that contain it, call your probation officer, attorney, or the court clerk to obtain it.

The rest of the box should be left blank at this time. Later on, when you get a hearing date, these items will be filled in.

FILL IN BOX 5

2. At the time of commission of the misdemeanor offense of *APRIL 17, 1980*, I was a minor, *17* years old.

The first portion of your petition informs the court that you meet the first requirement to use this procedure; that is, you were a minor at the time you committed the offense. Fill in the date you committed the offense and how old you were on that date. If you weren't a minor on that date, you may not use this procedure.

Terry remembers the date of the incident at the park. He fills in that date, and states he was 17 years old on that date.

FILL IN BOX 6

3. On *June 25, 1980*, I was convicted of the following misdemeanor offense(s) in this criminal court: *Assault (Penal Code Sec. 241a)*

Here, you put the date of your conviction and the actual offense for which you were convicted. In Terry's case, he learned from his probation papers that his conviction occurred on June 25, 1980, and that he was convicted for the crime of assault (Penal Code §241a). If he didn't have any papers, he could have obtained this information from his probation officer, his lawyer, or the court clerk.

Remember: The crime(s) you were convicted of may be different from the ones you were originally charged with. Your guilty plea may have been the result of a "plea bargain," where the original charges may have been reduced to a less serious offense. If your case went to trial, a jury or judge may have found you guilty of crimes different from those you were originally charged with.

Also, if you list more than one offense, contact a lawyer regarding your eligibility to seal your records using this procedure. If your conviction was for a crime classified as either a felony or an infraction, or for certain drug, sex, or automobile crimes, you may not use this procedure.

FILL IN BOX 7

4. ☒ I am eligible for relief provided by Penal Code §1203.4 and an application for that relief is attached.
    ☐ I am eligible for relief provided by Penal Code §1203.4a and an application for that relief is attached.
    ☐ I have previously received the relief provided for by either Penal Code §1203.4 or §1203.4a and an order for that relief is on file.

The petition to seal misdemeanor convictions of a minor can and should be used in connection with a petition to dismiss your case (described in Chapters 7 and 8). If you haven't applied to have your case dismissed previously, read Chapter 7 if you were put on probation, or Chapter 8 if you weren't. You should file the petition in either Chapter 7 or 8 at the same time that you file your petition to seal your misdemeanor conviction record. Both of these remedies will be heard by the court at the same time. In Terry's case, he checked the first box, since he was placed on probation. Had he not been placed on probation, he would have checked the second box.

FILL IN BOX 8

5. I have not been convicted of any other criminal offense except:
    ☒ None
    ☐ List date and offense(s) convicted of:

This portion of your petition informs the court that you haven't been convicted of other crimes since this case. If this is true, check the box before the word "None." If you've been convicted of any crimes since this case, you should check the box before the word "List," and list the date and crimes you've been convicted of.

Although there are some exceptions, other convictions will usually mean you're ineligible for this remedy. If so, talk to a lawyer to see whether there's a way around it. See Chapter 3(B)(1).

Terry hasn't been convicted of any other crimes since this incident in the park. He checks the box in front of the word "None."

FILL IN BOX 9

WHEREFORE, petitioner prays for an order, pursuant to Penal Code §1203.45:
☒ Sealing the record of conviction(s) and other official records in this case, including records of arrests resulting in these criminal proceedings;
☒ Sealing the records relating to other offenses charged in the accusatory pleadings of this case of which I was acquitted or the charges were dismissed.

This box is known as the "prayer," and is very much like the real thing. It informs the court of what you want to accomplish. If you were convicted of the only crime you were charged with, you should check the first box. If there were other charges that were dismissed, this record sealing law permits you to ask the court to seal all the records relating to those charges. In that situation, you should check the second box as well as the first box.

Terry wants the court to order his misdemeanor conviction records sealed, so he checks the first box. Since there are also records relating to the original felony charges, Terry can have those records sealed by checking the second box. If there hadn't been other charges, he wouldn't have checked the second box.

FILL IN BOX 10

I declare under penalty of perjury under the laws of the State of California
that the foregoing is true and correct.

DATED: *July 14, 1982*   *Jerry Thorn*
_____
                                                              DEFENDANT

In this box, you put the date you're filling out the petition and sign under penalty of perjury. This means that to the best of your knowledge, every statement that you made, and every statement made by the petition itself, is true. So long as you've done your best to provide accurate information, feel free to sign. If you're not sure whether some of the statements are true or not, do a little more homework. It's always better to leave something out than to include information that you know to be false, or that you aren't sure about.

Well, that's how you fill out a petition to have your misdemeanor records sealed. Not so bad, was it? And that's the most difficult part of the whole process.

Now, make sure you've detached the right form (the one with Penal Code §1203.45 and "application" on it), and fill it in as we've suggested in this section. Take your time.

Photocopy Note: Before you start filling out the form, it would be a very good idea to make a couple of copies, so in case you make a mistake, you'll have spares.

Steps 2-8

Now it's time to travel back to Chapter 7, Section E, Step 2 for further proceedings. Just remember that when you're filling out the Notice of Hearing form discussed in Chapter 7, check the third box for this remedy (§1203.45). If you're also filing a petition to dismiss your case, check either the first box (if you use the procedure described in Chapter 7) or the second box (if you use the procedure described in Chapter 8), in addition to the third box. You can use the one Notice of Hearing form to notify all the agencies that you want *both* the remedy in this chapter and the one in either Chapter 7 or 8.

Continue reading Steps 3-8 in Chapter 7. When you're finished, return to this chapter for the completion of your journey.

Step 9: Preparing Order Sealing Records

Welcome back from Chapter 7. You're here to stay. And this is the last step. Sometime before the hearing, you'll need to prepare the Order that the judge will sign, hopefully giving you what you ask for. If no hearing is required in your county, you should send or deliver this Order to the court clerk's office a short time after you file your petition. Be sure and attach a stamped, self-addressed envelope, so the court will send you a copy of the signed Order.

Turn to the Appendix and find a blank copy of the form included for your use, labelled "Order Sealing Misdemeanor Conviction and Other Records of Minor Offender (Penal Code §1203.45)." Make sure you have the right form before you tear it out. We recommend that you not fill it out until you've carefully read this section. After we've finished, fill the form out, make three copies, and take the original and three copies with you to court. When the judge grants your "prayer," he or she'll ask for the Order. If you don't have it prepared, it may mean a delay. If you don't plan to attend the hearing, make sure the original and three copies of the Order and a stamped self-addressed envelope are in the court on or before the hearing date.

FILL IN BOXES 1-4

Fill in the same as with the other documents.

FILL IN BOX 5

1. The petition to seal misdemeanor conviction and other records of a minor offender, under Penal Code §1203.45, filed on _____ came on for hearing as follows:
   a. Date: Dept: Div: Room:
   b. Judge (name):   ☐ Temporary
   c. ☐ Defendant present in court
   d. ☐ Defendant's attorney present in court (name):
   e. ☐ District Attorney/City Attorney present in court (name):
   f. ☐ Probation officer present in court (name):
   g. ☐

In this box, put the date you filed your petition and leave the rest of it blank. The court clerk will fill in these details.

FILL IN BOX 6

Copies of the notice of hearing and defendant's petition were served on all of the above-named offices.

2. ☐ Evidence presented to the court.

Leave this box blank. If anybody testifies in the hearing, the court clerk will check it.

FILL IN BOX 7

3. It appearing to the court from the records on file in this case, and from the defendant's petition and any information submitted by the District Attorney/ City Attorney and the Probation Department regarding this petition, that all of the allegations in the defendant's petition are true, defendant was a minor at the time of the commission of the misdemeanor offense of which he was convicted, and that this is a proper case for granting relief provided for in Penal Code §1203.45.

4. ☐ Order for Relief under Penal Code §1203.4/1203.4a is also signed by the court on this date.
   ☐ Order for Relief under Penal Code §1203.4/1203.4a was previously signed and filed on _____.

The third paragraph states the conclusion of the court that you qualify to have your case records sealed under this law. If you're also having a petition to dismiss your case (the procedures discussed in Chapter 7 and 8) heard at the same time as your petition to seal your misdemeanor conviction records, check the first box. If you previously had your case dismissed under either of those procedures, check the second box and fill in the date your case was ordered dismissed by the court. You should only check one of these two boxes.

FILL IN BOX 8

```
5.  IT IS ORDERED
    a.  ☐  All records, papers and exhibits in this case be sealed including the
           records of arrests resulting in these criminal proceedings.
        ☐  All records relating to other offenses charged in the complaint of which
           defendant was acquitted of the charges dismissed be sealed.
```

This portion of the Order lists what records are being sealed. This corresponds with the boxes checked on Box 9 of your petition. Check either one or both boxes, as you did on Box 9 of your petition.

FILL IN BOX 9

```
    b.  The clerk of this court, the county probation office, the following law
        enforcement agencies:

        the California Department of Justice, and all other governmental agencies,
        offices and officers seal such records as herein described in their custody
        or control and that the clerk enter this order accordingly.
    c.  This proceeding shall be deemed not to have occurred and the petitioner
        may answer accordingly to any question relating to their occurrence, pursuant
        to Penal Code §1203.45a.
```

The final paragraphs order the court clerk and all other agencies that have a copy of your record to seal those records. To this end, you should fill in the names of the police or other law enforcement agencies having records of your case. If you need more space, add an additional page.

Step 10:   Attend Court Hearing

At the time and place of the hearing on your petition, the judge will decide whether to grant or deny your request to get your misdemeanor conviction record sealed. The judge will review:

1) your petition (all the information about your case and your statements under penalty of perjury that you qualify to get your case dismissed),

2) the probation department's report, and

3) check to make sure the prosecuting attorney's office and the probation department have been notified about your petition and the hearing (from the Proof of Service).

If everything is in order, your request will be granted and the judge will sign the Order.

If you're required to attend the hearing, the judge may ask you, or the probation officer who prepared the criminal record investigation for the hearing, a few brief questions to make sure you really qualify. As long as you do (you stayed with us on our little trip earlier in the chapter), the questioning will be short and the Order will be signed.

If you're eligible to have your records sealed under this procedure, the judge will sign the Order and the court clerk will prepare a new "disposition report" on your case to notify the

Department of Justice in Sacramento that your records have been sealed. The Department will notify all police departments and law agencies who were notified of your original conviction to seal their records on your case this time.

If you don't attend the court hearing, you'll be sent a copy of the Order that shows the date it was signed and the name of the judge who signed it.

Follow-Up Note: Even though the Order is supposed to take care of everything, humans sometimes make mistakes. Especially where computers are involved, it's sometimes difficult to get information off a computer once it's been put on. Likewise, it's difficult to put it on when you need it most. For this reason, we strongly suggest you do a little follow-up about six months after the judge signs the Order. In Chapter 2, we tell you how to find out whether you have a record and to get a copy of it. Follow that procedure to see whether your record has really been changed. If not, take the steps suggested in that chapter to get the mistake corrected.

chapter 12

arrest records of juveniles treated as adults

IF YOU HAD YOUR CASE TRANSFERRED from juvenile court to criminal court and you were charged with, but not convicted of, a misdemeanor offense, you may be able to petition the court to have your record sealed.[1] The record sealing procedure described in this chapter applies to so few cases, that we haven't included any forms. If your case qualifies for this remedy, we suggest you contact a lawyer to prepare your petition. We do want to briefly describe the law, which is found in §851.7 of the Penal Code.

A. When Can This Procedure Be Used?

YOU CAN PETITION to have your arrest records sealed only if all of the following statements are true:

1. Age

At the time you were accused of committing the crime, you were a minor (under the age of 18, unless the offense was committed before March 7, 1973, in which case you were under the age of 21).

2. Type of Crime

The crime you were arrested for, and/or charged with, must be a misdemeanor crime and cannot include:

a. Sex offenses listed in §290 of the Penal Code, which requires registration;

b. Drug offenses starting in §11000 of the Health & Safety Code;

c. Automobile related offenses that violate state or local law relating to operating, stopping or parking a car.

If you were charged with any misdemeanor offense that falls within any of the subject areas mentioned above (2a-c), check with a lawyer to make sure you're eligible to use this remedy.

If you were arrested for, and charged with, any crime classified as either a felony or an infraction, you may not use this remedy.

---

[1]Penal Code §851.7.

3. Criminal Court

If criminal charges were filed, your case must have ended in criminal court. This means that your case was transferred from juvenile court to criminal court after a "fitness" hearing. If your case stayed in juvenile court, as the vast majority of misdemeanor cases do, or was in any federal court, this remedy won't apply to your case.

4. No Conviction

Your case must have ended without you being convicted of any crime. Your case may have ended at any of the following stages:

a. Charges Filed and Case Dismissed

After you were arrested by the police, the prosecuting attorney filed a petition in juvenile court and your case was transferred to criminal court. At your last court appearance, you were told that all criminal charges filed against you were dismissed.

b. Acquitted After Trial

A trial was held on the criminal charges filed against you and the jury's verdict (or in non-jury trials, the court's finding) wasn't guilty on all charges.

If your case ended with you being convicted of any crime, either by pleading guilty/no contest, or being found guilty after a trial, or if your trial ended because the jury couldn't decide on a verdict (hung jury), you may not use this remedy, unless all the criminal charges were eventually dismissed.

5. Prior Conviction in Criminal Court

The records of your case will only stay in the criminal court if you've been convicted in a criminal court or a different case. For example, if the records you want to seal are an arrest for a misdemeanor assault case (which was transferred from juvenile court to criminal court and the case ended with no conviction), and you were previously convicted in criminal court (not juvenile court) for driving under the influence of alcohol, then the record sealing procedure described in this chapter is the one for you.

If at the time your misdemeanor case is dismissed, you have *no* criminal court convictions on any other cases, the records of your dismissed misdemeanor criminal court case will be delivered back to the juvenile court and your name will be "obliterated" from "any index or minute book maintained in the criminal court." Once these records are returned to the juvenile court, you may have them sealed by using the procedure described in Chapter 4 (Welfare & Institutions Code §707.4).

You may only use the procedure described in this chapter if your case fits in all of the five qualifications listed above. If it does, contact a lawyer to prepare your petition.

B. Benefits of Sealing Misdemeanor Arrest Records

ONCE YOUR RECORDS ARE ORDERED sealed by the court, the record sealing law states "thereafter, the arrest, detention, and any further proceedings in the case shall be deemed not to have occurred," and you may answer accordingly any question relating to their occurrence.

chapter 13

honorable discharges from youth parole board

IF YOU WERE EVER SENTENCED to the California Youth Authority after being convicted of a crime, you may be able to get your conviction withdrawn and your case dismissed. The remedy described in this chapter only applies to a limited number of cases. Therefore, read the next several sections very carefully to make sure you qualify for these benefits.

A. Who Can Use This Procedure?

YOU CAN PETITION to have your conviction withdrawn and your case dismissed only if all the following statements are true:

- Your case ended in a California state adult criminal court. This means that if your case was handled entirely in juvenile court, federal court, or the courts of another state, you fail to qualify. Detour to Chapter 4 if your case stayed in juvenile court.
- You must have been convicted of a crime. If you plead guilty, or no contest, or were found guilty after a trial by judge or jury, you were convicted. Otherwise you weren't. Of course, if you were sentenced to the Youth Authority, the chances are excellent that you were in fact convicted of something.

- You must have been sentenced to the Youth Authority, without spending any time in regular jail or state prison.
- You must have received an honorable discharge from the Youth Authority after going through their program. This normally will be granted if you have a good parole record. The entity giving honorable discharge is called the Youthful Offender Parole Board.

B. When Can You Start Proceedings to Dismiss Your Case?

AS SOON AS YOU HAVE BEEN "honorably discharged" by the Youthful Offender Parole Board, you may petition the court to "set aside the verdict of guilty and dismiss the criminal charges filed against you." When you received your discharge, you should have been notified in writing about your opportunity to have your case dismissed.

C. Benefits of Getting Your Case Dismissed

ONCE YOUR CASE HAS BEEN ORDERED "dismissed" by the court, the law states you're thereafter "released from all penalties and disabilities resulting from any offense or crime . . . including, but not limited to, *any* disqualification for *any* employment or occupational license . . .created by *any* other provision of the law." The only exceptions to this release are: 1) if you were convicted of a felony, you still cannot own or possess a concealed firearm (*People v. Bell* (1989) 49 Cal.3d 502); 2) if you're applying to be a police officer, and you were convicted of a felony, you'll still be ineligible for the job (Government Code §1029; and 3) a dismissed conviction may be used to increase your punishment if you're later convicted of another crime (*People v. Jacob* (1985) 174 Cal.App.3d 1166). Convictions dismissed may not be brought up to discredit your testimony if you testify in another criminal case (*People v. Jackson* (1986) 177 Cal.App.3d 708).

D. How to Start the Procedure

FOR ALL PRACTICAL PURPOSES, there is little difference between the procedures used for the Chapter 7 remedy and this one. Since there are different legal authorities and qualifications for these two remedies, however, we have provided a separate chapter for this one. For certain information, we'll refer you back to Chapter 7 and then bring you back here for the rest of the procedures. This may seem a bit confusing, but if you carefully follow our instructions, there should be no problem.

Parole Department Note: The easiest and cheapest way to get your case dismissed is to have the parole department do it. Tell your parole officer you want his or her assistance to get your conviction dismissed under Welfare & Institutions Code §1772, the law which authorizes this remedy. Most parole officers will prepare all your forms and get your conviction dismissed, although you may have to fill out a questionnaire and be interviewed as part of the process.

If you think you would like to do it yourself, or no one will do it for you, this is where we provide specific step-by-step guidance. Don't let the thought of doing your own legal work scare you. Just be patient, follow our instructions, and when you're through, you'll be surprised how easy it was.

E. Which Court Forms to Use

SOME COUNTIES HAVE THEIR OWN printed form petitions which only require you to fill in the blanks, sign at the bottom and send them in. If such form petitions exist in your county (the county where your conviction occurred), you'll be able to find them at either 1) the criminal court clerk or 2) the parole department section which handles Youth Authority matters. Also, you might try the public defender's office. Some courts require you to use their forms, if they exist. Even if you don't have to, it's a good idea.

If there is no such form, however, we provide a form which is representative of the ones in use. Since our instructions apply to our own form, they may not be exactly what you need for the county, but they should prove helpful. So, whether you plan on using our form or the county's form, keep reading.

Turn to the Appendix and find the form called "Petition to Withdraw Conviction After Honorable Discharge From Youth Offender Parole Board, and For Relief From All Penalties and Disabilities Resulting from Offense (Welfare

& Institutions Code §1772)." While a lot of the language may seem like Greek, it actually asks for very little information. We'll tell you how to fill it in. Make sure you have the right form before you tear it out. We recommend you not fill it in until you've carefully read this section. However, if you want to do both at the same time, don't forget to make a photocopy first.

Step 1: Fill Out Petition

FILL IN BOX 1

```
┌────────────────────────────────────────────────────────────┐
│ ATTORNEY OR PARTY WITHOUT ATTORNEY (NAME AND ADDRESS)   TELEPHONE NO │
│                                                              │
│                                                              │
│                                                              │
│                                                              │
│ ATTORNEY FOR (NAME)                                          │
└────────────────────────────────────────────────────────────┘
```

Box 1 is for your name, current address and telephone number. If you represent yourself, put your name after "Defendant" and add the words "in pro per," which is Latin for "representing yourself."

FILL IN BOX 2

```
┌────────────────────────────────────────────────────────────┐
│            COURT OF CALIFORNIA, COUNTY OF                    │
│                              JUDICIAL DISTRICT               │
│      STREET ADDRESS                                          │
│      MAILING ADDRESS                                         │
│      CITY AND ZIP CODE                                       │
│      BRANCH NAME                                             │
└────────────────────────────────────────────────────────────┘
```

Box 2 contains the information about the court which you're asking to dismiss your conviction. If your conviction was for a misdemeanor, it was probably handled in municipal court. In most large counties, there are several municipal court judicial districts. If you don't know which one was involved in your case, call the court clerk and ask. Also, it might be found on any old court papers you may have kept. Finally, you can call your former probation officer or attorney. Fill in the word "municipal" before "court," the name of the county where your conviction occurred, after the words "County of," and the name of the judicial district on the second line, before the words "judicial district."

If your conviction was for a felony, it occurred in superior court. Superior courts are not divided into districts, but may have different branches. Find out what branch your superior court was and put it in after the words "Branch Name." Put the word "superior" before the word "court," and the name of the county where your conviction occurred after "County of."

This box also requires the address of the court. You can often find this in the phone book, or it may be on your old papers. The court clerk will also tell you over the phone. Make sure you get the correct address. If the mailing address is different than the street address (such as a P.O. Box), fill in both addresses.

FILL IN BOX 3

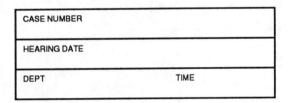

```
THE PEOPLE OF THE STATE OF CALIFORNIA
                 vs.

                              Defendant
```

This box contains the title of your case. Put your name after the "vs." If you go by more than one name, make sure you put the name your conviction occurred under. Otherwise, the court may get confused and problems may develop.

FILL IN BOX 4

```
CASE NUMBER

HEARING DATE

DEPT                        TIME
```

This box contains several items. The case number should be the same as it was on the case which resulted in your conviction. If you no longer remember, or don't have court papers which contain it, call your probation officer, attorney, or the court clerk to get it.

The rest of the box should be left blank at this time. Later on, when you get a hearing date, these items will be filled in.

FILL IN BOX 5

2. On _____, I was committed to the California Youth Authority by this court for a period prescribed by law.

Fill in the date you were committed to the California Youth Authority. This normally will be the date you were sentenced by the judge after you were convicted. If you don't know this information, ask your lawyer or parole officer.

FILL IN BOX 6

4. On _____, I was honorably discharged (my discharge was based upon my good record on parole) from control by the Youthful Offender Parole Board

Fill in the date you were "honorably discharged" by the Youthful Offender Parole Board.

FILL IN BOX 7

> WHEREFORE, petitioner prays for an order, pursuant to Welfare and Institutions Code §1772, that:
>
> 1. ☐ The court allow me to withdraw my plea of guilty/nolo contendere;
>
>   ☐ The court set aside and vacate the jury's verdict or the court's finding of guilty after the trial of the above-entitled action;
>
> 2. The court dismiss this action pursuant to Welfare and Institutions Code §1772.
>
> 3. The court order that I be released from all penalties and disabilities resulting from the offense or crime for which I was committed, including, but not limited to, any disqualification for any employment or occupational license, or both, created by any other provision of law.

This box is known as the "prayer." It informs the court of what you want. If your case ended with a guilty plea, check the first box. Most convictions result from guilty or no contest pleas, and the chances are pretty good that you'll be checking the first box also.

However, if your conviction resulted from a guilty verdict after trial by judge or jury, you'll want to check the second box.

Only check one of these two choices.

FILL IN BOX 8

> I declare under penalty of perjury under the laws of the State of California that the foregoing is true and correct.
>
> DATED: _____   _____
>   DEFENDANT

In this box, put the date you're filling out the petition, and sign under penalty of perjury. This means that to the best of your knowledge, every statement which you made, and every statement made by the petition itself, is true. So long as you have done your best to provide accurate information, feel free to sign. If you're not sure whether some of the statements are true or not, do a little more homework. It's always better to leave something out than to include information which you know to be false, or about which you aren't sure.

Well, that's how you fill out a petition to have your conviction dismissed. Not so bad, is it? And that's the most difficult part of the whole process.

At this time, take your form which says "Petition To Withdraw Conviction After Honorable Discharge From Youth Offender Parole Board, and for Relief From All Penalties And Disabilities Resulting From Offense (Welfare & Institutions Code §1772)" and fill it in as we've suggested in this section. Take your time.

Photocopy Note: Before you start filling out the form, it would be a very good idea to make a couple of copies, so in case you make a mistake, you'll have spares.

Step 2: Preparing Notice of Hearing

Before you go down to the courthouse to file your papers, you'll need to prepare a couple of additional forms. They're extremely easy, so long as you follow our step-by-step instructions.

The first of these forms is called a Notice of Hearing, which lets the necessary agencies know of your intentions to get your case dismissed. First, take a look at our form in the Appendix (Notice of Hearing/Proof of Service, Welfare & Institutions §1772).

FILL IN BOXES 1-4

The top part (Boxes 1-4) should look familiar. They're identical to the petition and should be filled out the same way.

FILL IN BOX 5

```
1. To ☐ _____  District Attorney for _____ County;
      ☐ _____  City Attorney for _____ City;
      ☐ _____  Youthful Offender Parole Board;
      ☐ _____  Probate Department _____ County;
```

In this box, you'll be listing the criminal justice agencies who are entitled to receive a copy of your petition and be notified of the hearing. The first agency to notify is the one which prosecuted you. In felony cases, this will be the district attorney of the county involved in your case. If your conviction was for a misdemeanor, the agency may be the city attorney's office instead of the district attorney. If you're unsure, check with your parole officer and/or your

attorney. If that doesn't work, call the court clerk and ask how you can find out.

If the district attorney prosecuted you, check the first box. If the city attorney prosecuted you, check the second box. Only one of these two choices should be selected.

The other agency which needs to be informed is the Youthful Offender Parole Board. Check the third box.

FILL IN BOX 6

```
    NOTICE is given that defendant _____ will move the
court for an order permitting defendant to withdraw conviction after
honorable discharge, from the Youthful Offender Parole Board, to dismiss the
case, and to release defendant from all penalties and disabilities resulting
from offense pursuant to Welfare and Institutions Code §1772.
```

Here, you put your name exactly as it appears on the Petition and Box 3 of this form.

FILL IN BOX 7

```
2. A hearing on this matter will be held as follows:
┌─────────────────────────────────────────────────────────────────────┐
│  a. date:      time:      in ☐ Dept:      ☐Div:      ☐ Room:          │
└─────────────────────────────────────────────────────────────────────┘
   b. Address of court:
```

This box tells the agencies when and where your hearing will take place. Since you're filling out this form before you file your petition, you have no idea what to put in. Don't worry. When you file your papers, you'll be able to fill in the

information at that time, or at some future time as indicated by the court clerk. The address for the court should be the same as you put in Box 2 of this form and your petition, *unless* the court has a different physical location from its mailing address. If you're not sure about this, call the court clerk and find out.

Now, if you haven't already done so, tear out the Notice of Hearing form which you found in the Appendix. First, turn it over. On the other side you'll see another form, called "Proof of Service." Leave that for now, and just fill in the Notice of Hearing side as we suggested.

Steps 3-8

At this point, it is time to turn to Chapter 7, Part E, and follow Steps 3-8 for further instructions. At the right time, we'll bring you back to this chapter for the final step.

Step 9: Prepare Order Dismissing Conviction

Welcome back from Chapter 7. Well, this is the last step. Sometime before the hearing, you'll need to prepare the Order which the judge will sign, hopefully giving you what you ask for. If no hearing was required in your county, you should send or deliver this Order to the court clerk's office a short time after you file your petition. Be sure to attach a stamped, self-addressed envelope, so the court will send you a copy of the signed Order.

Turn to the Appendix and find the form which says, "Order Permitting Defendant to Withdraw Conviction After Honorable Discharge From Youth Offender Parole Board and for Relief From all Penalties and Disabilities Resulting From Offense (Welfare & Institutions Code §1772)." Tear it out now, but don't fill lit in until you're through with our instructions.

FILL IN BOXES 1-4

Fill in the same as with the other documents.

FILL IN BOX 5

1. The application for relief under Welfare & Institutions Code §1772 filed on
   _____ came on for hearing as follows:
   a. Date: Dept: Div: Room:
   b. Judge (name):   ☐ Temporary
   c. ☐ Defendant present in court
   d. ☐ Defendant's attorney present in court (name):
   e. ☐ District Attorney/City Attorney present in court (name):
   f. ☐ Probation officer present in court (name):
   g. ☐

In this box, put the date you filed your petition and leave the rest of it blank. The court clerk will fill in those details.

FILL IN BOX 6

> Copies of the notice of hearing and defendant's petition were served on all
> of the above-named offices.
>
> 2. ☐   Evidence presented to the court.

Leave this box blank. If anybody testifies in
the hearing, the court clerk will check it.

FILL IN BOX 7

> 4. IT IS ORDERED
>   a. ☐   Defendant's plea of guilty/nolo contendere is withdrawn.
>   ☐   The jury's verdict or the court's finding of guilty after the trial of
>   the above-entitled action is set aside and vacated.
>   b. The case against defendant is hereby dismissed, pursuant to Welfare and
>   Institutions Code §1772.
>   c. The defendant is released from all penalties and disabilities resulting
>   from the offense(s) which he/she committed, including, but not limited
>   to, any disqualification for any employment or occupational license, or
>   both, created by another provision of law. However, defendant shall not
>   be eligible for appointment as a peace officer employed by any public
>   agency, other than the Department of the Youth Authority, if his or her
>   appointment would otherwise be prohibited by Government Code §1029.

If your conviction was the result of a plea,
check the first box. If your conviction was the
result of a trial, check the second box.
Remember, only one of these two boxes should
be checked, and this information should be the
same as the box you checked in Box 7 on your
petition.

The final paragraphs order that your case be
dismissed and that you be released from all
penalties and disabilities resulting from the
offense of which you were convicted. The Order
ends with the disclosure warning you that you
can't be hired as a policeman. Otherwise, you're
home free as far as employment or licensing
goes.

After you've filled in the above form, hold on
to it until the day of the hearing. Then make sure
you take it and four copies with you. When the
judge grants your "prayer," he'll ask for the
Order. If you don't have it prepared, it may mean
a delay. If you don't plan to attend the hearing,
make sure the original and four copies of the

Order and a stamped, self-addressed envelope
are in the court on or before the hearing date.

Step 10:   Attend Court Hearing

At the time and place of the hearing on your
petition, the judge will decide whether to grant or
deny your request to get your conviction
dismissed. The judge will:

1) review your petition (all the information
about your case and your statements under
penalty of perjury that you qualify to get your
case dismissed),

2) review the parole department's report, and

3) check to make sure the prosecuting
attorney's office and the parole department have
been notified about your petition and the hearing
(from the Proof of Service). If everything is in
order, your request will be granted and the judge
will sign the Order.

If you're required to attend the hearing, the
judge may ask you, or the parole officer who
prepared the criminal record investigation for the

hearing, a few brief questions to make sure you really qualify. As long as you do, the questioning will be short and the Order will be signed.

If you're eligible to have your case dismissed under this procedure, the judge will sign the Order and a new "disposition report" will be prepared so to put an additional entry on your criminal record that your case was dismissed pursuant to Welfare & Institutions Code §1772. If you didn't have to attend the court hearing, you'll be mailed a copy of the Order showing the date it was signed and the name of the judge who signed it.

Follow-Up Note: Even though the Order is supposed to take care of everything, humans sometimes make mistakes. We strongly suggest you do a little follow-up about six months after the judge signs the Order. In Chapter 2, we tell you how to find out whether you have a record and to get a copy of it. Follow that procedure.

F. Automatic Dismissal of Case After Honorable Discharge from CYA Correction School

THERE IS ONE OTHER LAW that is very similar to Welfare & Institutions Code §1772 and is found in §1179 of that same code. This law applied to you if you were sentenced to a California Youth Authority Correctional School. Your conviction will have been withdrawn and your case dismissed *automatically* (without your having to file a petition with the court) if *all* of the following are true:

- Your case ended in criminal court;
- You were convicted;
- You were sentenced to a California Youth Authority School;
- You stayed at this school until you were honorably dismissed or the full period of your commitment ended.

As soon as you were honorably dismissed or discharged after the full period of your commitment, the Youth Authority informed the court which sentenced you of your release. The court then automatically dismissed the criminal charges which were originally filed against you. Once these criminal charges were dismissed, you were "released from all penalties or disabilities resulting from the offenses." This "release from penalties" means you get the same benefits described in Section C of this chapter.

chapter 14 ─────────────────

rehabilitated
narcotics addicts

IN THIS LAST CHAPTER, we'll explain how the law permits rehabilitated narcotics addicts to get their criminal charges dismissed.[1] We don't include "how-to-do-it" forms for the procedure, since, if you're eligible, the procedure was probably done for you. We do want to explain who is eligible and what the benefits are if your charges were dismissed under the law (Welfare & Institutions Code §3200b).

A. Are You Eligible to Get Your Criminal Charges Dismissed?

IF YOU WERE EITHER ADDICTED to, or in "imminent danger of becoming" addicted to, narcotics when you were in criminal court, you may have been "treated" under special provisions of California law designed to "treat," not punish, narcotics addicts. Your court appearance may have been a sentencing hearing (after you were convicted of a crime), or a probation revocation hearing (probation from a prior criminal conviction). At that court hearing, if the judge concluded that you were, or were likely to become, an addict, you may have served your

time at a Narcotics Detention Treatment and Rehabilitation facility of the Department of Corrections.

The determination of whether you would serve your time at a treatment facility was made at a special superior court hearing. At least one, and sometimes two, doctors will have examined you and reported to the court if you were an addict. If the superior court hearing, after reviewing the doctor's reports and other evidence, concluded that you weren't an addict, or likely to become an addict, your case was returned for sentencing or probation revocation. If the superior court hearing concluded that you were addicted, or in "imminent danger of becoming" addicted to narcotics, then you may have been committed by the court to the custody of a treatment facility.

If your conviction was for certain violent felony charges, you weren't eligible for treatment. If during your "treatment," you exhibited "excessive criminality," you could have been found "unfit" for further treatment and would have been returned to the court for alternative sentencing (Welfare & Institutions Code §3052, 3).

After you were in a treatment facility and "recovered" from your addiction, you were

─────────────────────────────

[1]Welfare & Institutions Code §3200b

released by the Director of Corrections as an "outpatient."

If one year has passed and you haven't been released as an outpatient, your case will be reviewed to see if you should be released. As an "outpatient," you'll be closely supervised by the treatment facility. You may be asked to submit to periodic and surprise chemical tests to see if you've been using narcotics. If you've been using narcotics, you could be returned to the treatment facility (Welfare & Institutions Code §3152).

The maximum time you could be committed to spend in one of these treatment facilities is limited to the maximum term of jail or prison for the crime for which you were convicted (Welfare & Institutions Code §3201c).

Once you're an outpatient, you must not use any narcotics for a certain minimum time period if you want to have your case dismissed. Here are the time periods:

Time spent as an inpatient at the treatment facility	Minimum time during which you must not use narcotics
2 years or less	1 year
More than 2 years	16 months

During the minimum time during which you must not use narcotics, you need to comply with all the conditions of your release and the Director of Corrections must be of the opinion that you didn't use any narcotics during that time period. If the Director of Corrections believes that you're clean, he or she will advise the Narcotic Addict Evaluation Authority. If the Authority also agrees that you're clean, they'll file a "certificate" at the superior court that committed you to the treatment facility, which tells the court about your

successful treatment, and they'll ask the court to discharge you from the treatment program.

At the time that the court orders that you be discharged from the treatment program, the court may also modify your sentence, dismiss the criminal charges, or suspend further proceedings as it deems warranted "in the interest of justice." If your case started in municipal court, the judge of that court can decide if your case should be dismissed. Although it isn't required, the court does have the discretion or legal authority to dismiss all the criminal charges after you've successfully completed your treatment.

If you're not sure whether your case was dismissed, you can find out by either asking your lawyer, the Director of Corrections at the facility where you were treated, the person at the Narcotics Addict Evaluation Authority who processed your certificate, or the clerk of the court, to look up your case file and send you a copy of the last court order in your file. If you find that your case wasn't dismissed, you should ask your lawyer why it wasn't and whether you can ask the court to dismiss it now.

B. Benefits of Getting Your Case Dismissed

IF YOUR CASE WAS DISMISSED, that dismissal "shall have the same force and effect of a dismissal under Penal Code §1203.4, except the conviction is a prior conviction for the purposes of drug related charges" (Welfare & Institutions Code §3200b). To find out the benefits of getting your case dismissed, read Chapter 7, Section C.

Also, your dismissed conviction can no longer be used to disqualify you from being a peace officer. *Boyll vs. State Personnel Board* (1983) 146 Cal. App. [3d] 1070.

appendix

State of California
DEPARTMENT OF JUSTICE

APPLICATION TO OBTAIN COPY OF STATE SUMMARY CRIMINAL HISTORY RECORD

California Penal Code Sections 11120 through 11127 (see reverse side) afford persons concerning whom a State Summary Criminal History Record is maintained in the files of the California Bureau of Criminal Identification the opportunity to obtain a copy of the record compiled from such files and refute any erroneous or inaccurate information contained therein.

Submission of the requested information is necessary as it will be used to determine if a record exists. Failure to supply this information may prevent this agency from providing you with a copy of your record. This application will be retained in your record folder if one exists. The Chief of the Bureau of Criminal Identification, California Department of Justice, is responsible for the maintenance of the information. The mailing address is P.O. Box 903417, Sacramento, California, 94203-4170, telephone number (916) 739-5140.

Any criminal record existing concerning you will be forwarded via mail or other appropriate means agreed to by you and the Department.

The undersigned hereby applies to obtain a copy of his/her State Criminal History Record:

(TYPE OR PRINT)

Applicant's Name _____

                LAST NAME   FIRST NAME   MIDDLE NAME

Also known as
(or maiden name) _____

                LAST NAME   FIRST NAME   MIDDLE NAME

Mailing Address _____

                NUMBER   STREET

_____

                CITY   STATE   ZIP CODE

Date of Birth _____/_____/_____ Telephone Number _____

          MONTH DAY YEAR   (Area Code) (8 a.m. - 5 p.m.)

If you wish this record forwarded to someone other than yourself, or if you wish this record mailed to an address different than the one listed above, complete the following:

Name _____ Title _____

Mailing Address _____

                NUMBER   STREET

_____

                CITY   STATE   ZIP CODE

X _____ _____
SIGNATURE OF APPLICANT   DATE

A standard fingerprint form or fingerprint form BID-7 with the applicant's fingerprints imprinted theron, containing all requested information, must accompany this application.

A fee of twenty dollars ($20.00) in the form of a U.S. Money Order, Certified Check, or Cashier's Check made payable to the California Department of Justice must accompany this application when forwarded to the Department of Justice. If you are indigent, a declaration of inability to pay the required fee will be forwarded for your signature upon request.

BCID 8705 (Rev. 1/86)

11120. As used in this Article, "record" with respect to any person means the State summary criminal history information as defined in Subdivision (a) of Section 11105, maintained under such person's name by the Department of Justice.

11121. It is the function and intent of this Article to afford persons concerning whom a record is maintained in the files of the Bureau an opportunity to obtain a copy of the record compiled from such files, and to refute any erroneous or inaccurate information contained therein.

11122. Any person desiring a copy of the record relating to himself shall obtain an application form furnished by the Department which shall require his fingerprints in addition to such other information as the Department shall specify. Applications may be obtained from police departments, sheriff departments, or the Department of Justice. The fingerprinting agency may fix a reasonable fee for affixing the applicant's fingerprints to the form, and shall retain such fee.

11123. The applicant shall submit the completed application directly to the Department. The application shall be accompanied by a fee not to exceed twenty-five dollars ($25) that the Department determines equals the costs of processing the application and providing a copy of the record to the applicant. All fees received by the Department under this Section are hereby appropriated without regard to fiscal years for the support of the Department of Justice in addition to such other funds as may be appropriated therefor by the legislature. Any request for waiver of fee shall accompany the original request for the record and shall include a claim and proof of indigency.

11124. When an application is received by the Department, the Department shall determine whether a record pertaining to the applicant is maintained. If such record is maintained, the Department shall furnish a copy of the record to the applicant or to an individual designated by the applicant. If no such record is maintained, the Department shall so notify the applicant or an individual designated by the applicant. Delivery of the copy of the record, or notice of no record may be by mail or other appropriate means agreed to by the applicant and the Department.

11125. No person or agency shall require another person to obtain a copy of a record or notification that a record exists or does not exist, as provided in Section 11124, unless specifically authorized by law. A violation of this Section is a misdemeanor.

11126. (a) If the applicant desires to question the accuracy or completeness of any material matter contained in the record, he may submit a written request to the Department in a form established by it. The request shall include a statement of the alleged inaccuracy or incompleteness in the record, and its materiality, and shall specify any proof or corroboration available. Upon receipt of such request, the Department shall forward it to the person or agency which furnished the questioned information. Such person or agency shall, within 30 days of receipt of such written request for clarification, review its information and forward to the Department the results of such review.

(b) If such agency concurs in the allegations of inaccurateness or incompleteness in the record, and finds that the error is material, it shall correct its record and shall so inform the Department, which shall correct the record accordingly. The Department shall inform the applicant of its correction of the record under this Subdivision within 30 days. The Department and the agency shall notify all persons and agencies to which they have disseminated the incorrect record in the past 90 days of the correction of the record, and the applicant shall be informed that such notification has been given. The Department and the agency shall also notify those persons or agencies to which the incorrect record has been disseminated which have been specifically requested by the applicant to receive notification of the correction of the record, and the applicant shall be informed that such notification has been given.

(c) If such agency denies the allegations of inaccurateness or incompleteness in the record, the matter shall be referred for administrative adjudication in accordance with Chapter 5 (commencing with Section 11500) of Part I, Division 3, Title 2 of the Government Code for a determination of whether inaccuracy or incompleteness exists in the record. The agency from which the questioned information originated shall be the respondent in the hearing. If a material inaccuracy or incompleteness is found in any record, the agency in charge of that record shall be directed to correct it accordingly, and to inform the Department, which shall correct its record accordingly. The Department and the agency shall notify all persons and agencies to which they have disseminated the incorrect record in the past 90 days of the correction of the record, and the applicant shall be informed that such notification has been given. The Department and the agency shall also notify those persons or agencies to which the incorrect record has been disseminated which have been specifically requested by the applicant to receive notification of the correction of the record, and the applicant shall be informed that such notification has been given. Judicial review of the decision shall be governed by Section 11523 of the Government Code. The applicant shall be informed of the decision within 30 days of its issuance in accordance with Section 11518 of the Government Code.

11127. The Department shall adopt all regulations necessary to carry out the provisions of this Article.

Application and Declaration for Waiver of Fee
for Obtaining Criminal History Record

I, the undersigned, declare that I am unable to pay the fee to obtain a copy

of my criminal history record without impairing my obligation to meet the

common necessities of life.

I declare under penalty of perjury that the foregoing is true and correct and

was signed at _____, California, on _____,

19____.

_____

Declarant

BCID 8690

CLAIM OF ALLEGED INACCURACY OR INCOMPLETENESS

I have examined a copy of my California State Summary Criminal History Record as contained in the files of the Department of Justice, Bureau of Criminal Identification, and wish to take exception to its accuracy and/or completeness.

NAME _____

          LAST NAME   FIRST NAME   MIDDLE NAME

CII NUMBER _____ **DATE** _____

Complete a statement for each error or inaccuracy claimed. Use additional paper if necessary. Attach copies of any proof or corroboration available.

_____

_____

_____

_____

_____

_____

_____

_____

_____

_____

_____

SIGNATURE _____

Return this form to the attention of the Supervisor of the Record Review Unit at the California Department of Justice, Bureau of Criminal Identification, P.O. Box 903417, Sacramento, CA 94203-4170.

SUPERIOR **COURT OF CALIFORNIA, COUNTY OF**
SITTING AS THE JUVENILE COURT
STREET ADDRESS:
MAILING ADDRESS:
CITY AND ZIP CODE:
BRANCH NAME:

In the Matter of

Date of Birth: _____

PETITION FOR SEALING OF JUVENILE RECORDS

(Welfare & Inst. Sec. 781)

CASE NUMBER
HEARING DATE
DEPT   TIME

Petitioner, the undersigned, delares:

1. ☐ I am now at least 18 years old.
   ☐ 5 years or more have passed since the termination of Juvenile Court juris-
      diction, which occurred on or about _____.

2. I will be/was 38 years old on _____.

3. Yes   No   Part or all of this case involves violations of misdemeanor or
   ☐   ☐   infraction traffic laws.

4. I have not been convicted of any felonies or of any misdemeanors involving
   moral turpitude and rehabilitation has been attained.

5. I am informed and believe, and on that information and belief allege, that
   the following law enforcement agencies and public offices have custody of
   records, including records of arrest or detention, relating to this case:
   ☐ a. Clerk, Juvenile Court, in this county
   ☐ b. Probation Department in this county
   ☐ c. District Attorney's office in this county
   ☐ d. Public Defender's office in this county
   ☐ e. California Bureau of Criminal Identification, Department of Justice
   ☐ f. Federal Bureau of Investigation
   ☐ g. The following law enforcement agencies:

   ☐ h. Department of Motor Vehicles
   ☐ i. Others on attached list

   WHEREFORE, petitioner prays for an order that all records, papers, and exhibits in this case in the custody of the Juvenile Court, including the Juvenile
Court record, minute book entries, and entries on dockets, and other records
relating to the case in the custody of such other agencies and officials named
in this petition be sealed; that a copy of the order be sent to each agency and
official named in this petition ordering such agency and official to seal the
records in its custody and to destroy the sealed records
   ☐ in 5 years or
   ☐ when I am 38 years old,
and that the proceedings in this case shall be deemed never to have occurred.

(Continued on reverse)

I declare under penalty of perjury under the laws of the State of California that the foregoing is true and correct.

DATED: _____   _____

                                      PETITIONER

ATTORNEY OR PARTY WITHOUT ATTORNEY (NAME AND ADDRESS)	TELEPHONE NO.:	FOR COURT USE ONLY

ATTORNEY FOR (NAME):

SUPERIOR **COURT OF CALIFORNIA, COUNTY OF**
SITTING AS THE JUVENILE COURT
STREET ADDRESS:
MAILING ADDRESS:
CITY AND ZIP CODE:
BRANCH NAME:

In the Matter of

Date of Birth:

CASE NUMBER:

ORDER SEALING JUVENILE RECORDS

HEARING DATE:

(Welfare and Inst. Sec. 781)

DEPT.:   TIME:

1. The petition to seal juvenile records filed on _____
   came on for hearing as follows:
   a. Date: Dept: Div: Room:
   b. Judge (name):   ☐ Referee
   c. ☐ Petitioner present in court   ☐ Commissioner
   d. ☐ Petitioner's attorney present in court (name):
   e. ☐ District attorney present in court (name):
   f. ☐ Probation officer present in court (name):
   g. ☐
   The county probation department and the district attorney's office of this
   county were notified by this court of the filing of the petition.

2. ☐ Evidence presented to the court.

3. It appearing to the court from the records on file in this case and from the
   petition and any information submitted by the Probation Department and/or
   the District Attorney's office regarding this petition that all the allegations in the petition are true and that rehabilitation of the petitioner has
   been established to the satisfaction of this court and that petitioner is
   eligible to have the records of this case sealed.

4. IT IS ORDERED
   a. All records, papers, and exhibits of this case in the custody of this
      Juvenile Court, including the Juvenile Court records, minute book entries,
      and entries on dockets, and other records relating to this case, includ-
      ing records of arrest, fingerprints and photographs, in the custody of
      such other agencies and officials named below shall be sealed in such a
      manner that there remain no further indication that such record exists.
      ☐ Probation Department in this county
      ☐ District Attorney's office in this county
      ☐ Public Defender's office in this county
      ☐ California Bureau of Criminal Identification, Department of Justice
      ☐ Federal Bureau of Investigation
      ☐ The following law enforcement agencies:

      ☐ Department of Motor Vehicles
      ☐ Others on attached list

(Continued on reverse)

b. The clerk of this court shall transmit a certified copy of this order to each agency and official named in Paragraph 4a.

    i. Each of those agencies and officials shall seal the records in its custody as directed by this order, shall advise the court of compliance, and thereupon shall seal the copy of this order transmitted to it.

    ii. ☐ 5 years after sealing these records, each agency shall destroy the sealed records. (Welfare & Inst. Sec. 601 cases)

       ☐ On _____, the date when the petitioner is 38 years old, each agency shall destroy the sealed records. (Welfare & Inst. Sec. 602 cases)

    iii. Any agency which has forwarded information to the FBI is ordered to request that such information be returned to the agency so those records may be sealed pursuant to this order.

☐ c. If the petitioner was subject to the registration requirements set forth in Section 290 of the Penal Code, than the petitioner is now relieved from this registration requirement and all registration information in the custody of the Department of Justice and all other agencies and officials, which were named in paragraph 4a shall be destroyed.

d. The proceedings in this case shall be deemed never to have occurred, and the petitioner may properly reply accordingly to any inquiry about the events, records of which are ordered sealed.

DATED: _____

                                    JUDGE OF THE SUPERIOR COURT

ATTORNEY OR PARTY WITHOUT ATTORNEY (NAME AND ADDRESS)	TELEPHONE NO.:	FOR COURT USE ONLY

ATTORNEY FOR (NAME)

SUPERIOR **COURT OF CALIFORNIA, COUNTY OF**
SITTING AS THE JUVENILE COURT
STREET ADDRESS:
MAILING ADDRESS:
CITY AND ZIP CODE:
BRANCH NAME:

In the Matter of

Date of Birth:

CASE NUMBER

PETITION FOR SEALING OF JUVENILE RECORDS

HEARING DATE:

(Welfare & Inst. Sec. 389)

DEPT.:   TIME

Petitioner, the undersigned, declares:

1. ☐ I am now at least 18 years old.
   ☐ 5 years or more have passed since the termination of Juvenile Court jurisdiction, which occurred on or about _____.

2. I have not been convicted of any felonies or of any misdemeanors involving
   moral turpitude and rehabilitation has been attained.

3. I am informed and believe, and on that information and belief allege, that
   the following law enforcement agencies and public offices have custody of my
   records, including records of arrest or detention, relating to this case:
   ☐ a. Clerk, Juvenile Court, in this county
   ☐ b. Probation Department in this county
   ☐ c. District Attorney's office in this county
   ☐ d. Public Defender's office in this county
   ☐ e. The following law enforcement agencies:

   ☐ f. Others on attached list

   WHEREFORE, petitioner prays for an order that all records, papers, and exhibits in this case in the custody of the Juvenile Court, including the Juvenile
Court record, minute book entries, and entries on dockets, and other records
relating to the case in the custody of such other agencies and officials named
in this petition be sealed; that a copy of the order be sent to each agency and
official named in this petition ordering such agency and official to seal the
records in its custody and to destroy the sealed records in 5 years; and that
the proceedings in this case shall be deemed never to have occurred.

   I declare under penalty of perjury under the laws of the State of California
that the foregoing is true and correct.

DATED:

_____
PETITIONER

ATTORNEY OR PARTY WITHOUT ATTORNEY (NAME AND ADDRESS)	TELEPHONE NO.:	FOR COURT USE ONLY
ATTORNEY FOR (NAME):		

SUPERIOR **COURT OF CALIFORNIA, COUNTY OF**
SITTING AS THE JUVENILE COURT
STREET ADDRESS:
MAILING ADDRESS:
CITY AND ZIP CODE:
BRANCH NAME:

In the Matter of

Date of Birth:

CASE NUMBER:

ORDER SEALING JUVENILE RECORDS

HEARING DATE:

DEPT.:   TIME:

(Welfare & Inst. Sec. 389)

1. The petition to seal juvenile records filed on _____ came
   on for hearing as follows:
   a. Date: Dept: Div: Room:
   b. Judge (name):   ☐ Referee
   c. ☐ Petitioner present in court   ☐ Commissioner
   d. ☐ Petitioner's attorney present in court (name):
   e. ☐ District attorney present in court (name):
   f. ☐ Probation officer present in court (name):
   g. ☐
   The county probation department and the district attorney's office of this
   county were notified by this court of the filing of the petition.

2. ☐ Evidence presented to the court.

3. It appearing to the court from the records on file in this case and from the
   petition and any information submitted by the Probation Department and/or
   the District Attorney's office regarding this petition that all the allegations in the petition are true and that rehabilitation of the petitioner
   has been established to the satisfaction of this court and that petitioner
   is eligible to have the records of this case sealed, pursuant to Welfare
   & Inst. Sec. 389.

4. IT IS ORDERED
   a. All records, papers and exhibits of this case in the custody of this
      Juvenile Court, including the Juvenile Court records, minute book
      entries, and entries on dockets, and other records relating to this case,
      including records of arrest, fingerprints and photographs, in the custody
      of such other agencies and officials named below shall be sealed in such
      a manner that there remain no further indication that such record exists.
      ☐ Probation Department in this county
      ☐ District Attorney's office in this county
      ☐ Public Defender's office in this county
      ☐ The following law enforcement agencies:

      ☐ Others on the attached list

(Continued on reverse)

b. The clerk of this court shall transmit a certified copy of this order to each agency and official named in Paragraph 4a.
   i. Each of these agencies and officials shall seal the records in its custody as directed by this order, shall advise the court of compliance, and there upon shall seal the copy of this order transmitted to it.
   ii. 5 years after sealing these records, each agency shall destroy the sealed records.
   iii. Any agency which has forwarded information to the F.B.I. is ordered to request that such information be returned to the agency so those records may be sealed pursuant to this order.
c. The proceedings in this case shall be deemed never to have occurred and the petitioner may properly reply accordingly to any inquiry about the events, records of which are ordered seals.

DATED:

_____
JUDGE OF THE SUPERIOR COURT

ATTORNEY OR PARTY WITHOUT ATTORNEY (NAME AND ADDRESS)	TELEPHONE NO.:	FOR COURT USE ONLY
ATTORNEY FOR (NAME)		

COURT OF CALIFORNIA, COUNTY OF

STREET ADDRESS:
MAILING ADDRESS: JUDICIAL DISTRICT
CITY AND ZIP CODE:
BRANCH NAME:

THE PEOPLE OF THE STATE OF CALIFORNIA
                          vs.

                                          Defendant

APPLICATION TO WITHDRAW CONVICTION, TO DISMISS THE CASE, AND FOR RELIEF FROM ALL PENALTIES AND DISABILITIES RESULTING FROM OFFENSE (Penal Code Sec. 1203.4)	CASE NUMBER: HEARING DATE: DEPT: TIME:

I, the undersigned applicant, declare:

1. I am the defendant in the above-entitled criminal action.

2. On _____, I was convicted of the following offense(s):

3. As a result of that conviction, I was put on probation for a time period of __ years __ months.

4. ☐ My period of probation ended on _____.
   ☐ I was discharged from probation, prior to the termination of my probation period, by an order of this court, on _____.
   ☐ I request that I be granted the relief available under Penal Code Sec. 1203.4, even though my probation has not ended, in the interests of justice, because of the following reasons:

5. During the entire period I was on probation, I fulfilled all of the conditions of probation.

6. I am not now serving a sentence for any other criminal offense.

7. I am not now on probation for any other criminal offense.

8. I am not now charged with the commission of any offense in any pending criminal case.

WHEREFORE, applicant moves that:

1. ☐ The court allow me to withdraw my plea of guilty/nolo contendere and to enter a plea of not guilty;
   ☐ The court set aside and vacate the jury's verdict or the court's finding of guilty after the trial of the above-entitled action;

(Continued on reverse)

2. The court dismiss this action pursuant to Penal Code Sec. 1203.4.

3. The court order that I be released from all penalties and disabilities resulting from the conviction(s) except as otherwise expressly provided by law.

I declare under penalty of perjury under the laws of the State of California that the foregoing is true and correct.

DATED: _____   _____ _____

                                                                            DEFENDANT

ATTORNEY OR PARTY WITHOUT ATTORNEY (NAME AND ADDRESS)	TELEPHONE NO.:	FOR COURT USE ONLY

ATTORNEY FOR (NAME)

COURT OF CALIFORNIA, COUNTY OF

STREET ADDRESS:
MAILING ADDRESS: JUDICIAL DISTRICT
CITY AND ZIP CODE:
BRANCH NAME:

THE PEOPLE OF THE STATE OF CALIFORNIA
           vs.

                          Defendant

CASE NUMBER:
HEARING DATE:
DEPT.:   TIME:

ORDER PERMITTING DEFENDANT TO WITHDRAW CONVICTION, TO DISMISS
THE CASE, AND TO RELEASE DEFENDANT FROM ALL PENALTIES AND DIS-
ABILITIES RESULTING FROM OFFENSE
                (Penal Code Sec. 1203.4)

1. The application for relief under Penal Code Sec. 1203.4 filed on
   _____ came on for hearing as follows:
   a. Date: Dept: Div: Room:
   b. Judge (name):   ☐ Temporary
   c. ☐ Defendant present in court
   d. ☐ Defendant's attorney present in court (name):
   e. ☐ District Attorney/City Attorney present in court (name):
   f. ☐ Probation officer present in court (name):
   g. ☐
   Copies of the notice of hearing and defendant's application were served on
   all of the above-named offices.

2. ☐ Evidence presented to the court.

3. It appearing to the court from the records on file in this case, and from the
   defendant's application and any information submitted by the District Attorney/
   City Attorney and the Probation Department regarding this application, that
   all of the allegations in the defendant's application are true and that
   defendant is eligible for the relief provided for in Penal Code Sec. 1203.4.

4. IT IS ORDERED
   a. ☐ Defendant's plea of guilty/nolo contendere is withdrawn and a plea of
      not guilty is entered.
      ☐ The jury's verdict or the court's finding of guilty after the trial of
      the above-entitled action is set aside and vacated.
   b. The case against defendant is hereby dismissed, pursuant to Penal Code
      Sec. 1203.4.
   c. The defendant is released from all penalties and disabilities resulting
      from the offense(s) of which he/she was convicted, except as otherwise
      expressly provided by law.
      (Applicant is informed that this order does not relieve him/her of the
      obligation to disclose this conviction(s) in response to any direct
      question contained in any questionnaire or application for public office,
      for license by any state or local agency, or for contracting with the
      California State Lottery).

DATED:

_____
                JUDGE

ATTORNEY OR PARTY WITHOUT ATTORNEY (NAME AND ADDRESS)	TELEPHONE NO.:	FOR COURT USE ONLY

ATTORNEY FOR (NAME)

COURT OF CALIFORNIA, COUNTY OF

STREET ADDRESS: JUDICIAL DISTRICT
MAILING ADDRESS:
CITY AND ZIP CODE:
BRANCH NAME

THE PEOPLE OF THE STATE OF CALIFORNIA
           vs.

                          Defendant

CASE NUMBER:

APPLICATION TO WITHDRAW MISDEMEANOR CONVICTION AFTER ONE YEAR WITHOUT PROBATION, TO DISMISS THE CASE, AND FOR RELIEF FROM ALL PENALTIES AND DISABILITIES RESULTING FROM OFFENSE
(Penal Code Sec. 1203.4a)

HEARING DATE:

DEPT: TIME

I, the undersigned applicant, declare:

1. I am the defendant in the above-entitled criminal action.

2. On _____, I was convicted of the following misdemeanor offense(s):

3. I was not put on probation and I have fully complied with and performed the sentence of the court.

4. More than one year has passed since the date of pronouncement of judgment.

5. I am not now serving a sentence for any other criminal offense.

6. I am not now charged with the commission of any offense in any pending criminal case.

7. Since the date of pronouncement of judgment, I have lived an honest and upright life and have conformed to and obeyed the laws of the land.

WHEREFORE, applicant moves that:

1. ☐ The court allow me to withdraw my plea of guilty/nolo contendere and to enter a plea of not guilty;
   ☐ The court set aside and vacate the jury's verdict or the court's finding of guilty after the trial of the above-entitled action;

2. The court dismiss this action pursuant to Penal Code Sec. 1203.4a.

3. The court order that I be released from all penalties and disabilities resulting from the conviction(s) except as otherwise expressly provided by law.

I declare under penalty of perjury under the laws of the State of California that the foregoing is true and correct.

DATED: _____

                              _____
                                        DEFENDANT

ATTORNEY OR PARTY WITHOUT ATTORNEY (NAME AND ADDRESS)	TELEPHONE NO.:	FOR COURT USE ONLY

ATTORNEY FOR (NAME):

COURT OF CALIFORNIA, COUNTY OF

STREET ADDRESS:
MAILING ADDRESS: JUDICIAL DISTRICT
CITY AND ZIP CODE:
BRANCH NAME:

THE PEOPLE OF THE STATE OF CALIFORNIA
     vs.

              Defendant

ORDER PERMITTING DEFENDANT TO WITHDRAW MISDEMEANOR CONVICTION
AFTER ONE YEAR WITHOUT PROBATION, TO DISMISS THE CASE, AND TO
RELEASE DEFENDANT FROM ALL PENALTIES AND DISABILITIES
RESULTING FROM OFFENSE   (Penal Code Sec. 1203.4a)

CASE NUMBER:

HEARING DATE:

DEPT: TIME:

1. The application for relief under Penal Code Sec. 1203.4a filed on
   _____ came on for hearing as follows:
   a. Date: Dept: Div: Room:
   b. Judge (name):   ☐ Temporary
   c. ☐ Defendant present in court
   d. ☐ Defendant's attorney present in court (name):
   e. ☐ District Attorney/City Attorney present in court (name):
   f. ☐ Probation officer present in court (name):
   g. ☐
   Copies of the notice of hearing and defendant's application were served on
   all of the above-named offices.

2. ☐ Evidence presented to the court.

3. It appearing to the court from the records on file in this case, and from the
   defendant's application and any information submitted by the District Attorney/
   City Attorney and the Probation Department regarding this application, that
   all of the allegations in the defendant's application are true and that
   defendant is eligible for the relief provided for in Penal Code Sec. 1203.4a.

4. IT IS ORDERED
   a. ☐ Defendant's plea of guilty/nolo contendere is withdrawn and a plea of
      not guilty is entered.
      ☐ The jury's verdict or the court's finding of guilty after the trial of
      the above-entitled action is set aside and vacated.
   b. The case against defendant is hereby dismissed, pursuant to Penal Code
      Sec. 1203.4a.
   c. The defendant is released from all penalties and disabilities resulting
      from the offense(s) of which he/she was convicted, except as otherwise
      expressly provided by law.

DATED: _____

             _____
                   JUDGE

SUPERIOR COURT OF CALIFORNIA, COUNTY OF

STREET ADDRESS:
MAILING ADDRESS:
CITY AND ZIP CODE:
BRANCH NAME:

THE PEOPLE OF THE STATE OF CALIFORNIA
            vs.

                                            Defendant

CASE NUMBER:
HEARING DATE:
DEPT.   TIME:

APPLICATION OF DEFENDANT FOR THE COURT TO DECLARE THE OFFENSE
FOR WHICH HE/SHE WAS CONVICTED A MISDEMEANOR AFTER PROBATION
ENDS; ORDER
                    (Penal Code Sec. 17 b 3)

I, the undersigned applicant, declare:

1. I am the defendant in the above-entitled criminal action.

2. On _____, I was convicted of the following felony
   offense(s):

   This crime is punishable by imprisonment in prison, county jail, or fine.

3. As a result of that conviction, I was put on probation and my period of probation ended on _____.

4. During the entire period I was on probation, I fulfilled all of the conditions of probation.

   WHEREFORE, applicant requests that the court declare this offense(s) to be
a misdemeanor(s).

   I declare under penalty of perjury under the laws of the State of California
that the foregoing is true and correct.

DATED: _____
                                          DEFENDANT

                    ORDER DECLARING OFFENSE TO BE MISDEMEANOR

1. The application that the court declare this offense(s) to be misdemeanor(s)
   under Penal Code Sec. 17 b 3 came on for hearing as follows:
   a. Date: Dept: Div: Room:
   b. Judge (name):   Temporary
   c. ☐ Defendant present in court
   d. ☐ Defendant's attorney present in court (name):
   e. ☐ District Attorney present in court (name):
   f. ☐ Probation officer present in court (name):
   g. ☐
   Copies of the notice of hearing and defendant's application were served on
   all of the above-named offices.

                        (Continued on reverse)

2. It appearing to the court from the records on file in this case, and from the defendant's application and any information submitted by the District Attorney and the Probation Department regarding this application, that defendant is eligible to have this offense declared a misdemeanor.

3. The court declares that the offense(s) listed above on the application of the defendant is/are to be misdemeanor(s).

4. Pursuant to Penal Code Sec. 13151, this court shall furnish a disposition report to the Department of Justice and to the law enforcement agency which had primary jurisdiction to investigate the offense alleged in the complaint which informs them of the terms of this order.

DATED: _____

_____

JUDGE OF THE SUPERIOR COURT

ATTORNEY OR PARTY WITHOUT ATTORNEY (NAME AND ADDRESS)	TELEPHONE NO.:	FOR COURT USE ONLY

ATTORNEY FOR (NAME)

COURT OF CALIFORNIA, COUNTY OF

STREET ADDRESS: JUDICIAL DISTRICT

MAILING ADDRESS

CITY AND ZIP CODE

BRANCH NAME

THE PEOPLE OF THE STATE OF CALIFORNIA

vs.

Defendant

CASE NUMBER:

PETITION TO SEAL MINOR'S RECORDS OF MISDEMEANOR CONVICTION IN CRIMINAL COURT AND OTHER RECORDS OF OFFENSE
(Penal Code Sec. 1203.45)

HEARING DATE:

DEPT.:   TIME:

I, the undersigned petitioner declare:

1. I am the defendant in the above-entitled criminal action.

2. At the time of commission of the misdemeanor offense of _____,
   I was a minor, ____ years old.

3. On _____, I was convicted of the following misdemeanor
   offense(s) in this criminal court:

4. ☐ I am eligible for relief provided by Penal Code Sec. 1203.4 and an applica-
      tion for that relief is attached.
   ☐ I am eligible for relief provided by Penal Code Sec. 1203.4a and an appli-
      cation for that relief is attached.
   ☐ I have previously received the relief provided for by either Penal Code
      Sec. 1203.4 or Sec. 1203.4a and an order for that relief is on file.

5. I have not been convicted of any other criminal offense except:
   ☐ None
   ☐ List date and offense(s) convicted of:

WHEREFORE, petitioner prays for an order, pursuant to Penal Code Sec. 1203.45:
☐ Sealing the record of conviction(s) and other official records in this
   case, including records of arrests resulting in these criminal proceedings;
☐ Sealing the records relating to other offenses charged in the accusatory
   pleadings of this case of which I was acquitted or the charges were dismissed.

I declare under penalty of perjury under the laws of the State of California
that the foregoing is true and correct.

DATED: _____
                                              DEFENDANT

ATTORNEY OR PARTY WITHOUT ATTORNEY (NAME AND ADDRESS)	TELEPHONE NO.:	FOR COURT USE ONLY
ATTORNEY FOR (NAME)		

COURT OF CALIFORNIA, COUNTY OF

JUDICIAL DISTRICT

STREET ADDRESS:
MAILING ADDRESS:
CITY AND ZIP CODE:
BRANCH NAME:

THE PEOPLE OF THE STATE OF CALIFORNIA
vs.

Defendant

CASE NUMBER:

ORDER SEALING MISDEMEANOR CONVICTION AND OTHER RECORDS OF MINOR OFFENDER

(Penal Code Sec. 1203.45)

HEARING DATE:

DEPT   TIME

1. The petition to seal misdemeanor conviction and other records of a minor offender under Penal Code Sec. 1203.45, filed on _____ came on for hearing as follows:
   a. Date: Dept: Div: Room:
   b. Judge (name):   ☐ Temporary
   c. ☐ Defendant present in court
   d. ☐ Defendant's attorney present in court (name):
   e. ☐ District Attorney/City Attorney present in court (name):
   f. ☐ Probation officer present in court (name):
   g. ☐
   Copies of the notice of hearing and defendant's petition were served on all of the above-named offices.

2. ☐ Evidence presented to the court.

3. It appearing to the court from the records on file in this case, and from the defendant's petition and any information submitted by the District Attorney/City Attorney and the Probation Department regarding this petition, that all of the allegations in the defendant's petition are true, defendant was a minor at the time of the commission of the misdemeanor offense of which he was convicted, and that this is a proper case for granting relief provided for in Penal Code Sec. 1203.45.

4. ☐ Order for Relief under Penal Code Sec. 1203.4/1203.4a is also signed by the court on this date.
   ☐ Order for Relief under Penal Code Sec. 1203.4/1203.4a was previously signed and filed on _____.

5. IT IS ORDERED
   a. ☐ All records, papers and exhibits in this case be sealed including the records of arrests resulting in these criminal proceedings.
   ☐ All records relating to other offenses charged in the complaint of which defendant was acquitted of the charges dismissed be sealed.
   b. The clerk of this court, the county probation office, the following law enforcement agencies:

(Continued on reverse)

the California Department of Justice, and all other governmental agencies, offices and officers seal such records as herein described in their custody or control and that the clerk enter this order accordingly.

c. This proceeding shall be deemed not to have occurred and the petitioner may answer accordingly to any question relating to their occurrence, pursuant to Penal Code Sec. 1203.45a.

DATED: _____   _____

                                                                    JUDGE

ATTORNEY OR PARTY WITHOUT ATTORNEY (NAME AND ADDRESS)	TELEPHONE NO.:	FOR COURT USE ONLY

ATTORNEY FOR (NAME)

COURT OF CALIFORNIA, COUNTY OF

STREET ADDRESS: JUDICIAL DISTRICT

MAILING ADDRESS:

CITY AND ZIP CODE:

BRANCH NAME:

THE PEOPLE OF THE STATE OF CALIFORNIA

vs.

Defendant

CASE NUMBER:

PETITION TO WITHDRAW CONVICTION AFTER HONORABLE DISCHARGE FROM YOUTHFUL OFFENDER PAROLE BOARD, TO DISMISS THE CASE, AND FOR RELIEF FROM ALL PENALTIES AND DISABILITIES RESULTING FROM OFFENSE   (Welfare & Inst. Sec. 1772)

HEARING DATE:

DEPT: TIME:

I, the undersigned defendant, declare:

1. I am the defendant in the above-entitled criminal action.

2. On _____, I was committed to the California Youth Authority by this court for a period prescribed by law.

3. During the period of my control by the California Youth Authority, I was not placed in State Prison.

4. On _____, I was honorably discharged (my discharge was based upon my good record on parole) from control by the Youthful Offender Parole Board.

WHEREFORE, petitioner prays for an order, pursuant to Welfare and Institutions Sec. 1772, that:

1. ☐ The court allow me to withdraw my plea of guilty/nolo contendere;
   ☐ The court set aside and vacate the jury's verdict or the court's finding of guilty after the trial of the above-entitled action;

2. The court dismiss this action pursuant to Welfare and Institutions Sec. 1772.

3. The court order that I be released from all penalties and disabilities result- ing from the offense or crime for which I was committed, including, but not limited to, any disqualification for any employment or occupational license, or both, created by any other provision of law.

I declare under penalty of perjury under the laws of the State of California that the foregoing is true and correct.

DATED: _____
                                                          DEFENDANT

ATTORNEY OR PARTY WITHOUT ATTORNEY (NAME AND ADDRESS)	TELEPHONE NO.:	FOR COURT USE ONLY

ATTORNEY FOR (NAME)

COURT OF CALIFORNIA, COUNTY OF

STREET ADDRESS:
MAILING ADDRESS: JUDICIAL DISTRICT
CITY AND ZIP CODE:
BRANCH NAME

THE PEOPLE OF THE STATE OF CALIFORNIA
             vs.

                      Defendant

CASE NUMBER

NOTICE OF HEARING
PROOF OF SERVICE

HEARING DATE:

DEPT: TIME

1. To ☐ _____ District Attorney for _____ County;
   ☐ _____ City Attorney for _____ City;
   ☐ _____ Probation Department _____ County;

   NOTICE is given that defendant _____
   will move the court for an order:

   ☐ permitting defendant to withdraw or set aside his/her conviction, to dismiss the case, and for relief from all penalties and disabilities pursuant
   to Penal Code Sec. 1203.4;

   ☐ permitting defendant to withdraw or set aside his/her conviction, to
   dismiss the case, and for relief from all penalties and disabilities
   pursuant to Penal Code Sec. 1203.4a;

   ☐ permitting minor defendant to seal records of misdemeanor conviction in
   criminal court and other records of offense, pursuant to Penal Code Sec.
   1203.45;

   ☐ to reduce the offense from a felony to a misdemeanor, pursuant to Penal
   Code Sec. 17.

2. A hearing on this matter will be held as follows:

a. date:	time:	in ☐ Dept:	☐ Div:	☐ Room:

   b. Address of court:

3. This hearing will be based on this notice, the attached declaration of
   defendant, the papers and records on file herein, and such oral and docu-
   mentary evidence as may be presented at the hearing.

(Proof of Service is on the back)

PROOF OF SERVICE

PROOF OF PERSONAL SERVICE

☐

I am over the age of 18 and not a party to this case. I am a resident of or employed in the county of _____. My residence or business address is:

I served the foregoing Notice of Hearing by personally delivering a true copy of the Notice of Hearing and defendant's declaration to each person whose name and address is given below on the date of _____.

I declare under penalty of perjury under the laws of the State of California that the foregoing is true and correct.

_____   _____
(Print name)   (Sign name)

PROOF OF SERVICE BY MAIL

☐

I am over the age of 18 and not a party to this cause. I am a resident of or employed in the county where the mailing occurred. My residence or business address is:

I served the foregoing Notice of Hearing and Declaration by enclosing a true copy in a sealed envelope addressed to each person whose name and address is given below and depositing the envelope in the United States mail with the postage fully prepaid.

(1) Date of deposit: _____   (2) Place of deposit (city & state):

I declare under penalty of perjury under the laws of the State of California that the foregoing is true and correct.

(date): _____   at (place): _____ , California

_____   _____
(Type or Print Name)   (Signature of Declarant)

NAME AND ADDRESS OF EACH PERSON TO WHOM NOTICE WAS MAILED OR DELIVERED:

ATTORNEY OR PARTY WITHOUT ATTORNEY (NAME AND ADDRESS)	TELEPHONE NO.:	FOR COURT USE ONLY

ATTORNEY FOR (NAME)

COURT OF CALIFORNIA, COUNTY OF

JUDICIAL DISTRICT

STREET ADDRESS:
MAILING ADDRESS:
CITY AND ZIP CODE:
BRANCH NAME:

THE PEOPLE OF THE STATE OF CALIFORNIA
        vs.

                             Defendant

ORDER PERMITTING DEFENDANT TO WITHDRAW CONVICTION AFTER
HONORABLE DISCHARGE (YOPB), TO DISMISS THE CASE, AND TO
RELEASE DEFENDANT FROM ALL PENALTIES AND DISABILITIES
RESULTING FROM OFFENSE   (Welfare and Inst. Sec. 1772)

CASE NUMBER:

HEARING DATE:

DEPT: TIME:

1. The petition for relief under Welfare and Institutions Code Sec. 1772 filed
   _____ came on for hearing as follows:
   a. Date: Dept: Div: Room:
   b. Judge (name):   ☐ Temporary
   c. ☐ Defendant present in court
   d. ☐ Defendant's attorney present in court (name):
   e. ☐ District Attorney/City Attorney present in court (name):
   f. ☐ Probation officer present in court (name):
   g. ☐
   Copies of the notice of hearing and defendant's petition were served on
   all of the above-named offices.

2. ☐ Evidence presented to the court.

3. It appearing to the court from the records on file in this case, and from
   the defendant's petition and any information submitted by the District
   Attorney/City Attorney and the Probation Department regarding this petition,
   that all of the allegations in the defendant's petition are true and that
   defendant is eligible for the relief provided for in Welfare and Institutions
   Code Sec. 1772.

4. IT IS ORDERED
   a. ☐ Defendant's plea of guilty/nolo contendere is withdrawn.
      ☐ The jury's verdict or the court's finding of guilty after the trial of
         the above-entitled action is set aside and vacated.
   b. The case against defendant is hereby dismissed, pursuant to Welfare and
      Institutions Code Sec. 1772.
   c. The defendant is released from all penalties and disabilities resulting
      from the offense(s) which he/she committed, including, but not limited
      to, any disqualification for any employment or occupational license, or
      both, created by any other provision of law. However, defendant shall not
      be eligible for appointment as a peace officer employed by any public
      agency, other than the Department of the Youth Authority, if his or her
      appointment would otherwise be prohibited by Government Code Sec. 1029.

DATED: _____

                                    _____
                                            JUDGE

BUREAU OF IDENTIFICATION

𝔇epartment of 𝔍ustice

3301 C STREET

TO APPLICANT:

Health and Safety Code (H&S) Section 11361.5(b) states that if prior to January 1, 1976 you have a record of conviction(s) and/or an arrest(s) not followed by conviction for violations of H&S 11357, 11364, 11365, 11550 or their predecessors, you may apply to the Department of Justice for destruction of record(s) in connection with these offenses. If you meet the requirements for arrest record destruction, complete the following application.

APPLICATION TO DESTROY ARREST/CONVICTION RECORDS
(Health and Safety Code Section 11361.5(b))

TYPE OR PRINT THE FOLLOWING INFORMATION:

Applicant:	Last Name	First	Middle
Also Known As:	Last Name	First	Middle
Address: Number	Street		Apt. No.
City		State	Zip Code
Telephone:	Business	Residence	
Date of Birth:	Month Day Year		
Signature:		Date	

Mail this application with a fee of $37.50 (in the form of a U.S. Money Order, certified check or cashier's check made payable to the Department of Justice) to:

> Department of Justice
> Bureau of Identification
> P.O. Box 903417
> Sacramento, California 94203-4170

IMPORTANT: See reverse side for additional information pertaining to Health and Safety Code Section 11361.5(b) and optional information.

HEALTH AND SAFETY CODE SECTION 11361.5(b) STATES IN PART:
  "The department may request, but not require, the applicant to include a self-administered fingerprint upon the application. If the department is unable to sufficiently identify the applicant for purposes of this subdivision without such fingerprint or without additional fingerprints, it shall so notify the applicant and shall request the applicant to submit such fingerprints as may be required to effect identification, including a complete set if necessary, or, alternatively, to abandon the application and request a refund of all or a portion of the fee submitted with the application as provided in this section. If the applicant fails or refuses to submit fingerprints in accordance with the department's request within such reasonable time as shall be established by the department, or if the applicant requests a refund of the fee, the department shall promptly mail a refund to the applicant at the address specified in the application or at such other address as may be specified by the applicant. However, if the department has notified the applicant that election to abandon the application will result in forfeiture of a specified amount which is a portion of the fee, the department may retain such portion of the fee as the department may determine will defray the actual costs of processing the application, provided the amount of such portion retained shall not exceed ten dollars ($10.00)."

The Department of Justice has determined that upon notification an applicant shall submit fingerprints within 15 days of such notification. If the applicant does not respond to the notification within 15 days, or chooses not to submit fingerprints and abandons further pursuit of the application, the applicant will forfeit $10.00 to the department to defray processing costs. The remaining fee will be refunded.

THE FOLLOWING INFORMATION IS OPTIONAL. COMPLETION WILL EXPEDITE THE PROCESSING OF YOUR APPLICATION.

SELF-ADMINISTERED
RIGHT INDEX FINGERPRINT

DATE OF ARREST	ARRESTING AGENCY	

Social Security No.: _____   Driver's License No.: _____

FOR DEPARTMENTAL USE ONLY

Certificate of Compliance

☐ No record located for this application.

☐ The application has been fully complied with as of this date.

_____   _____
        Signature   Date

AGENCY NOTIFICATION:

1. _____   3. _____

2. _____   4. _____

SELF-HELP LAW BOOKS & SOFTWARE

SOFTWARE

willmaker
Nolo Press/Legisoft
Recent statistics say chances are better than 2 to 1 that you haven't written a will, even though you know you should. WillMaker makes the job easy, leading you step by step in a fill-in-the-blank format. Once you've gone through the program, you print out the will and sign it in front of witnesses. Because writing a will is only one step in the estate planning process, WillMaker comes with a 200-page manual providing an overview of probate avoidance and tax planning techniques.
National 3rd Ed.
Apple, IBM PC 5 1/4 & 3 1/2, Macintosh $59.95

california incorporator
Attorney Mancuso and Legisoft, Inc.
About half of the small California corporations formed today are done without the services of a lawyer. This easy-to-use software program lets you do the paperwork with minimum effort. Just answer the questions on the screen, and California Incorporator will print out the 35-40 pages of documents you need to make your California corporation legal.
California 1st Ed. (IBM PC 5 1/4 & 3 1/2) $129.00

the california nonprofit corporation handbook—computer edition with disk
Attorney Anthony Mancuso
This is the standard work on how to form a nonprofit corporation in California. Included on the disk are the forms for the Articles, Bylaws and Minutes you will need, as well as regular and special director and member minute forms. Also included are line-by-line instructions explaining how to apply for and obtain federal tax exempt status—this critical step applies to incorporating in all 50 states.
California 1st Ed.
Macintosh, IBM PC 5 1/4 & 3 1/2 $69.00

how to form your own texas corporation—computer edition with disk
AttorneyAnthony Mancuso

how to form your own new york corporation—computer edition with disk
AttorneyAnthony Mancuso
More and more business people are incorporating to qualify for tax benefits, limited liability status, the benefit of employee status and financial flexibility. These software packages contain all the instructions, tax information and forms you need to incorporate a small business. All organizational forms are on disk.
1st Edition
Macintosh, IBM PC 5 1/4 & 3 1/2 $69.00

for the record
Attorney Warner & Pladsen
A book/software package that helps to keep track of personal and financial records; create documents to give to family members in case of emergency; leave an accurate record for heirs, and allows easy access to all important records with the ability to print out any section.
National 1st Ed.
Macintosh, IBM PC 5 1/4 & 3 1/2 $49.95

ESTATE PLANNING & PROBATE

nolo's simple will book
Attorney Denis Clifford
We feel it's important to remind people that if they don't make arrangements before they die, the state will give their property to certain close family members. If you want a particular person to receive a particular object, you need a will. It's easy to write a legally valid will using this book.
National 2nd Ed. $17.95

plan your estate: wills, probate avoidance, trusts & taxes
Attorney Denis Clifford
A will is only one part of an estate plan. The first concern is avoiding probate so that your heirs won't receive a greatly diminished inheritance years later. This book shows you how to create a "living trust" and gives you the information you need to make sure whatever you have saved goes to your heirs, not to lawyers and the government.
National 1st Ed. $17.95

the power of attorney book
Attorney Denis Clifford
The Power of Attorney Book concerns something you've heard about but probably would rather ignore: Who will take care of your affairs, make your financial and medical decisions, if you can't? With this book you can appoint someone you trust to carry out your wishes.
National 3rd Ed. $19.95

how to probate an estate
Julia Nissley
When a close relative dies, amidst the grieving there are financial and legal details to be dealt with. The natural response is to rely on an attorney, but that response can be costly. With How to Probate an Estate, you can have the satisfaction of doing the work yourself and saving those fees.
California 4th Ed. $24.95

the california nonprofit corporation handbook

Attorney Anthony Mancuso

Used by arts groups, educators, social service agencies, medical programs, environmentalists and many others, this book explains all the legal formalities involved in forming and operating a nonprofit corporation. Included are all the forms for the Articles, Bylaws and Minutes you will need. Also included are complete instructions for obtaining federal 501(c)(3) exemptions and benefits. The tax information in this section applies wherever your corporation is formed.

California 5th Ed. $29.95

how to form your own corporation

Attorney Anthony Mancuso

More and more business people are incorporating to qualify for tax benefits, limited liability status, the benefit of employee status and the financial flexibility. These books contain the forms, instructions and tax information you need to incorporate a small business.

California 7th Ed.	$29.95
Texas 4th Ed.	$24.95
New York 2nd. Ed.	$24.95
Florida 2nd Ed.	$24.95

california professional corporation handbook

Attorney Anthony Mancuso

Health care professionals, marriage, family and child counsellors, lawyers, accountants and members of certain other professions must fulfill special requirements when forming a corporation in California. This edition contains up-to-date tax information plus all the forms and instructions necessary to form a California professional corporation. An appendix explains the special rules that apply to each profession.

California 4th Ed. $34.95

marketing without advertising

Michael Phillips & Salli Rasberry

Every small business person knows that the best marketing plan encourages customer loyalty and personal recommendation. Phillips and Rasberry outline practical steps for building and expanding a small business without spending a lot of money.

National 1st Ed. $14.00

the partnership book

Attorneys Clifford & Warner

Lots of people dream of going into business with a friend. The best way to keep that dream from turning into a nightmare is to have a solid partnership agreement. This book shows how to write an agreement that covers evaluation of partner assets, disputes, buy-outs and the death of a partner.

National 3rd Ed. $18.95

nolo's small business start-up

Mike McKeever

Should you start a business? Should you raise money to expand your already running business? If the answers are yes, this book will show you how to write an effective business plan and loan package.

National 3rd Ed. $17.95

the independent paralegal's handbook: how to provide legal services without going to jail

Attorney Ralph Warner

A large percentage of routine legal work in this country is performed by typists, secretaries, researchers and various other law office helpers generally labeled paralegals. For those who would like to take these services out of the law office and offer them at a reasonable fee in an independent business, attorney Ralph Warner provides both legal and business guidelines.

National 1st Ed. $12.95

getting started as an independent paralegal (two audio tapes)

Attorney Ralph Warner

This set of tapes is a carefully edited version of Nolo Press founder Ralph Warner's Saturday Morning Law School class. It is designed for people who wish to go into business helping consumers prepare their own paperwork in uncontested actions such as bankruptcy, divorce, small business incorporations, landlord-tenant actions, probate, etc. Also covered are how to set up, run, and market your business, as well as a detailed discussion of Unauthorized Practice of Law.

National 1st Ed. $24.95

devil's advocates: the unnatural history of lawyers

Jonathan & Andrew Roth

This book is a painless and hilarious education on the legal profession from its rude beginning through its ruder history to its rudest present. Laugh or weep as you learn the historical underpinnings of how and why lawyers have solidly become their own worst enemies.

1st Ed. $12.95

29 reasons not to go to law school

Ralph Warner & Toni Ihara

Lawyers, law students, their spouses and consorts will love this little book with its zingy comments and Thurberesque cartoons, humorously zapping the life of the law.—Peninsula Times Tribune Filled with humor and piercing observations, this book can save you three years, $70,000 and your sanity.

3rd Ed. $9.95

poetic justice

Ed. by Jonathan & Andrew Roth

A unique compilation of humorous quotes about lawyers and the legal system, from Socrates to Woody Allen. $8.95

how to file for bankruptcy

Attorneys Stephen Elias, Robin Leonard & Albin Renauer
Here we show you how to decide whether or not filing for bankruptcy makes sense and if it does, we give you step-by-step instructions as to how to do it. *How To File For Bankruptcy* covers the procedure for completing a Chapter 7 and includes a discussion of Chapter 13 to help you decide which process is appropriate for you.
National 1st Ed. $24.95

collect your court judgment

Scott, Elias & Goldoftas
After you win a judgment in small claims, municipal or superior court, you still have to collect your money. Here are step-by-step instructions on how to collect your judgment from the debtor's bank accounts, wages, business receipts, real estate or other assets.
California 1st Ed. $24.95

simple contracts for everyday use

Attorney Stephen Elias
Here are clearly written legal form contracts to: buy and sell property, borrow and lend money, store and lend personal property, make deposits on goods for later purchase, release others from personal liability, or pay a contractor to do home repairs.
National 1st Ed. $12.95

social security, medicare & pensions: a sourcebook for older americans

Attorney Joseph L. Matthews & Dorothy Matthews Berman
Social security, medicare and medicaid programs follow a host of complicated rules. Those over 55, or those caring for someone over 55, will find this comprehensive guidebook invaluable for understanding and utilizing their rightful benefits. A special chapter deals with age discrimination in employment and what to do about it.
National 4th Ed. $15.95

everybody's guide to small claims court

Attorney Ralph Warner
So, the dry cleaner ruined your good flannel suit. Your roof leaks every time it rains, and the contractor who supposedly fixed it won't call you back. The bicycle shop hasn't paid for the tire pumps you sold it six months ago. This book will help you decide if you have a case, show you how to file and serve papers, tell you what to bring to court, and how to collect a judgment.
California 8th Ed. $14.95
National 4th Ed. $14.95

for sale by owner

George Devine
In 1986 about 600,000 homes were sold in California at a median price of $130,000. Most sellers worked with a broker and paid the 6% commission. For the median home that meant $7,800. Obviously, that's money that could be saved if you sell your own house. This book provides the background information and legal technicalities you will need to do the job yourself and with confidence.
California 1st Ed. $24.95

homestead your house

Attorneys Warner, Sherman & Ihara
Under California homestead laws, up to $60,000 of the equity in your home may be safe from creditors. But to get the maximum legal protection you should file a Declaration of Homestead before a judgment lien is recorded against you. This book includes complete instructions and tear-out forms.
California 7th Ed. $9.95

the landlord's law book: vol. 1, rights & responsibilities

Attorneys Brown & Warner
Every landlord should know the basics of landlord-tenant law. In short, the era when a landlord could substitute common sense for a detailed knowledge of the law is gone forever. This volume covers: deposits, leases and rental agreements, inspections (tenants' privacy rights), habitability (rent withholding), ending a tenancy, liability, and rent control.
California 2nd Ed. $24.95

the landlord's law book: vol. 2, evictions

Attorney David Brown
Even the most scrupulous landlord may sometimes need to evict a tenant. In the past it has been necessary to hire a lawyer and pay a high fee. Using this book you can handle most evictions yourself safely and economically.
California 2nd Ed. $24.95

tenants' rights

Attorneys Moskowitz & Warner
Your "security building" doesn't have a working lock on the front door. Is your landlord liable? How can you get him to fix it? Under what circumstances can you withhold rent? When is an apartment not "habitable?" This book explains the best way to handle your relationship with your landlord and your legal rights when you find yourself in disagreement.
California 10th Ed. $15.95

the deeds book: how to transfer title to california real estate

Attorney Mary Randolph
If you own real estate, you'll almost surely need to sign a new deed at one time or another. *The Deeds Book* shows you how to choose the right kind of deed, how to complete the tear-out forms, and how to record them in the county recorder's public records.
California 1st Ed. $15.95

dog law

Attorney Mary Randolph

There are 50 million dogs in the United States—and, it seems, at least that many rules and regulations for their owners to abide by. *Dog Law* covers topics that everyone who owns a dog, or lives near one, needs to know about disputes, injury or nuisance.

National 1st Ed. $12.95

the criminal records book

Attorney Warren Siegel

We've all done something illegal. If you were one of those who got caught, your juvenile or criminal court record can complicate your life years later. The good news is that in many cases your record can either be completely expunged or lessened in severity. *The Criminal Records Book* takes you step by step through the procedures to: seal criminal records, dismiss convictions, destroy marijuana records, reduce felony convictions.

California 2nd Ed. $14.95

draft, registration and the law

Attorney R. Charles Johnson

This clearly written guidebook explains the present draft law and how registration (required of all male citizens within thirty days of their eighteenth birthday) works. Every available option is presented along with a description of how a draft would work if there were a call tomorrow.

National 2nd Ed. $9.95

fight your ticket

Attorney David Brown

At a trade show in San Francisco recently, a traffic court judge (who must remain nameless) told our associate publisher that he keeps this book by his bench for easy reference.

If you think that ticket was unfair, here's the book showing you what to do to fight it.

California 3rd Ed. $16.95

how to become a united states citizen

Sally Abel Schreuder

This bilingual (English/Spanish) book presents the forms, applications and instructions for naturalization. This step-by-step guide will provide information and answers for legally admitted aliens who wish to become citizens.

National 3rd Ed. $12.95

how to change your name

Attorneys Loeb & Brown

Wish that you had gone back to your maiden name after the divorce? Tired of spelling over the phone V-e-n-k-a-t-a-r-a-m-a-n S-u-b-r-a-m-a-n-i-a-m?

This book explains how to change your name legally and provides all the necessary court forms with detailed instructions on how to fill them out.

California 5th Ed. $19.95

legal research: how to find and understand the law

Attorney Stephen Elias

Legal Research could also be called Volume-Two-for-all-Nolo-Press-Self-Help-Law-Books. A valuable tool for paralegals, law students and legal secretaries, this book provides access to legal information—the legal self-helper can find and research a case, read statutes, and make Freedom of Information Act requests.

National 2nd Ed. $14.95

family law dictionary

Attorneys Leonard and Elias

Written in plain English (as opposed to legalese), the Family Law Dictionary has been compiled to help the lay person doing research in the area of family law (i.e., marriage, divorce, adoption, etc.). Using cross referencs and examples as well as definitions, this book is unique as a reference tool.

National 1st Edition $13.95

patent, copyright & trademark: intellectual property law dictionary

Attorney Stephen Elias

This book uses simple language free of legal jargon to define and explain the intricacies of items associated with trade secrets, copyrights, trademarks and unfair competition, patents and patent procedures, and contracts and warranties.—IEEE Spectrum

If you're dealing with any multi-media product, a new business product or trade secret, you need this book.

National 1st Ed. $17.95

the living together kit

Attorneys Ihara & Warner
Few unmarried couples understand the laws that may affect them. Here are useful tips on living together agreements, paternity agreements, estate planning, and buying real estate.
National 6th Ed. $17.95

how to do your own divorce

Attorney Charles E. Sherman
This is the book that launched Nolo Press and advanced the self-help law movement. During the past 17 years, over 400,000 copies have been sold, saving consumers at least $50 million in legal fees (assuming 100,000 have each saved $500—certainly a conservative estimate).
California 15th Ed. $14.95
Texas 2nd Ed. (Sherman & Simons) $14.95

california marriage & divorce law

Attorneys Warner, Ihara & Elias
For a generation, this practical handbook has been the best resource for the Californian who wants to understand marriage and divorce laws. Even if you hire a lawyer to help you with a divorce, it's essential that you learn your basic legal rights and responsibilities.
California 10th Ed. $18.95

practical divorce solutions

Attorney Charles Ed Sherman
Written by the author of *How to Do Your Own Divorce* (with over 500,000 copies in print), this book provides a valuable guide both to the emotional process involved in divorce as well as the legal and financial decisions that have to be made.
California 1st Ed. $12.95

how to modify and collect child support in california

Attorneys Matthews, Siegel & Willis
California has established landmark new standards in setting and collecting child support. Payments must now be based on both objective need standards and the parents' combined income. Using this book, custodial parents can determine if they are entitled to higher child support payments and can implement the procedures to obtain that support.
California 2nd Ed. $17.95

the guardianship book

Lisa Goldoftas & Attorney David Brown
Thousands of children in California are left without a guardian because their parents have died, abandoned them or are unable to care for them. *The Guardianship Book* provides step-by-step instructions and the forms needed to obtain a legal guardianship without a lawyer.
California 1st Ed. $19.95

a legal guide for lesbian and gay couples

Attorneys Curry & Clifford
A Legal Guide contains crucial information on the special problems facing lesbians and gay men with children, civil rights legislation, and medical/legal issues.
National 5th Ed. $17.95

how to adopt your stepchild in california

Frank Zagone & Attorney Mary Randolph
For many families that include stepchildren, adoption is a satisfying way to guarantee the family a solid legal footing. This book provides sample forms and complete step-by-step instructions for completing a simple uncontested adoption by a stepparent.
California 3rd Ed. $19.95

how to copyright software

Attorney M.J. Salone
Copyrighting is the best protection for any software. This book explains how to get a copyright and what a copyright can protect.
National 3rd Ed. $34.95

the inventor's notebook

Fred Grissom & Attorney David Pressman
The best protection for your patent is adequate records. The Inventor's Notebook provides forms, instructions, references to relevant areas of patent law, a bibliography of legal and non-legal aids, and more. It helps you document the activities that are normally part of successful independent inventing.
National 1st Ed. $19.95

legal care for your software

Attorneys Daniel Remer & Stephen Elias
If you write programs you intend to sell, or work for a software house that pays you for programming, you should buy this book. If you are a freelance programmer doing software development, you should buy this book.—Interface
This step-by-step guide for computer software writers covers copyright laws, trade secret protection, contracts, license agreements, trademarks, patents and more.
National 3rd Ed. $29.95

patent it yourself

Attorney David Pressman
You've invented something, or you're working on it, or you're planning to start...Patent It Yourself offers help in evaluating patentability, marketability and the protective documentation you should have. If you file your own patent application using this book, you can save from $1500 to $3500.
National 2nd Ed. $29.95

nolo

SELF-HELP LAW BOOKS & SOFTWARE

ORDER FORM

Quantity	Title	Unit Price	Total

Sales Tax (CA residents only):

7 1/4% Alameda, Contra Costa, San Diego, San Mateo & Santa Clara counties

6 3/4% Fresno, Inyo, LA, Sacramento, San Benito, San Francisco & Santa Cruz counties

6 1/4% All others

Subtotal _____

Sales Tax _____

TOTAL _____

Method of Payment:

☐ Check enclosed

☐ VISA   ☐ Mastercard

Acct # _____ Exp. _____

Signature _____

Phone (____) _____

Ship to:

Name _____

Address _____

_____

For faster service, use your credit card and our toll-free numbers:

Monday-Friday 9-5 Pacific Time

US		1-800-992-6656
CA	(outside 415 area)	1-800-445-6656
	(inside 415 area)	1-415-549-1976
General Information		**1-415-549-1976**

Mail to:

NOLO PRESS
950 Parker Street
Berkeley CA 94710

Prices subject to change

Please allow 1-2 weeks for delivery

Delivery is by UPS; no P.O. boxes, please

ORDER DIRECT AND WE PAY POSTAGE & HANDLING!

Two Years Free!

Nolo Press wants you to have top quality and up-to-date legal information. The **Nolo News**, our "Access to Law" quarterly newspaper, contains an update section which will keep you abreast of any changes in the law relevant to **The Criminal Records Book**. You'll find interesting articles on a number of legal topics, book reviews and our ever-popular lawyer joke column.

Send in the registration card below and receive FREE a two-year subscription to the **Nolo News** (normally $12.00). Your subscription will begin with the first quarterly issue published after we receive your card.

NOLO PRESS
The Criminal Records Book Registration Card

We would like to hear from you. Please let us know if the book met your needs. Fill out and return this card for a FREE two-year subscription to the *Nolo News* (if you have already paid for a subscription, we will extend it for two years). In addition, we'll notify you when we publish a new edition of **The Criminal Records Book.** (This offer is good in the U.S.only.)

Name _____

Address _____

City _____ State _____ Zip _____

Your occupation_____

Briefly, for what purpose did you use this book?

_____

_____

Did you find the information in the book helpful?
 (extremely helpful) 1 2 3 4 5 (not at all)

Where did you hear about the book? _____

Did you consult a lawyer?_____

Have you used other Nolo books?____Yes, ____No

Where did you buy the book? _____

Suggestions for improvement: _____

_____

_____

_____

_____

_____

_____

_____

_____

_____

_____

_____

_____

Nolo books are]…"written in plain language, free of legal mumbo jumbo, and spiced with witty personal observations."
—ASSSOCIATED PRESS

"Well-produced and slickly written, the [Nolo] books are designed to take the mystery out of seemingly involved procedures, carefully avoiding legalese and leading the reader step-by-step through such everyday legal problems as filling out forms, making up contracts, and even how to behave in court."
—SAN FRANCISCO EXAMINER

"…Nolo publications…"guide people simply through the how, when, where and why of law."
—WASHINGTON POST

fold --

affix
postage
here

_____

NOLO PRESS
950 Parker St.
Berkeley, CA 94710

fold --

"Increasingly, people who are not lawyers are performing tasks usually regarded as legal work…And consumers, using books like Nolo's, do routine legal work themselves."

"…All of [Nolo's] books are easy-to-understand, are updated regularly, provide pull-out forms…and are often quite moving in their sense of compassion for the struggles of the lay reader."
—SAN FRANCISCO CHRONICLE